BLACK&DECKER®

THE COMPLETE GUIDE TO

DIY PROJECTS FOR
LUXURIOUS LIVING

Adding Style & Elegance
with Showcase Features You Can Build

By Jerri Farris

Creative Publishing
international

MINNEAPOLIS, MINNESOTA
www.creativepub.com

**Creative Publishing
international**

Copyright © 2008
Creative Publishing international, Inc.
400 First Avenue North
Suite 300
Minneapolis, Minnesota 55401
1-800-328-3895
www.creativepub.com
All rights reserved

Printed at R.R. Donnelley

10 9 8 7 6 5 4 3 2 1

Library of Congress Cataloging-in-Publication Data

Farris, Jerri.
  The complete guide to DIY projects for luxurious living : adding style
& elegance with showcase features you can build / by Jerri Farris.
     p. cm. -- (Complete guide)
  At head of title: Branded by Black & Decker
  Summary: "Features a collection of high-end home improvement projects
designed for do-it-yourselfers"--Provided by publisher.
  Includes index.
  ISBN-13: 978-1-58923-336-2 (pbk.)
  ISBN-10: 1-58923-336-0 (pbk.)
  1. Recreation rooms--Design and construction--Amateurs' manuals. 2.
Dwellings--Maintenance and repair--Amateurs' manuals. 3. Do-it-yourself
work. I. Black & Decker Corporation (Towson, Md.) II. Title. III.
Title: Branded by Black & Decker. IV. Title: Complete guide to
do-it-yourself projects for luxurious living. V. Series.

  TH4815.F37 2008
  643'.7--dc22

2007039144

President/CEO: Ken Fund
VP for Sales & Marketing: Peter Ackroyd

Home Improvement Group

Publisher: Bryan Trandem
Managing Editor: Tracy Stanley
Senior Editor: Mark Johanson
Editor: Jennifer Gehlhar

Creative Director: Michele Lanci-Altomare
Senior Design Manager: Brad Springer
Design Managers: Jon Simpson, Mary Rohl

Lead Photographer: Steve Galvin
Photo Coordinator: Joanne Wawra
Shop Manager: Bryan McLain
Shop Assistant: Cesar Fernandez Rodriguez

Production Managers: Linda Halls, Laura Hokkanen

Author: Jerri Farris
Page Layout Artist: Danielle Smith
Photographers: Andrea Rugg, Joel Schnell, Mark Hardy
Shop Help: Lyle Ferguson, David Hartley, Scott Boyd

The Complete Guide to DIY Projects for Luxurious Living
Created by: The Editors of Creative Publishing international, Inc., in cooperation with Black & Decker.
Black & Decker® is a trademark of The Black & Decker Corporation and is used under license.

NOTICE TO READERS

For safety, use caution, care, and good judgment when following the procedures described in this book. The publisher and Black & Decker cannot assume responsibility for any damage to property or injury to persons as a result of misuse of the information provided.

The techniques shown in this book are general techniques for various applications. In some instances, additional techniques not shown in this book may be required. Always follow manufacturers' instructions included with products, since deviating from the directions may void warranties. The projects in this book vary widely as to skill levels required: some may not be appropriate for all do-it-yourselfers, and some may require professional help.

Consult your local building department for information on building permits, codes, and other laws as they apply to your project.

Contents

The Complete Guide
to DIY Projects for
Luxurious Living

Introduction

Most of us wouldn't actually want to trade lives with the rich and famous, but we can't deny our fascination with their lifestyles, their toys, and their homes. For generations, movies have given us glimpses of how the other half lives. Now, we watch television shows that play out against the background of incredible mansions and let us peek through the tall hedges and see behind the closed doors of homes owned by the wealthy.

Among other things, we've discovered that we want to come home at the end of a long day and soak in a huge tub or work out in our own gym or fire up a cigar in an elegant room. We want to incorporate some luxury into our living. And that brings us to this book, *DIY Projects for Luxurious Living.* In the following pages, you're going to find ideas and projects that will help you transform an ordinary room into a luxurious environment. We think you'll be surprised at how easy it can be to spruce up your space.

Before we go any further, let's explore exactly what *luxury* means. In real estate terminology, a "luxury home" is one priced over one million dollars, but true luxury is not about the price or even the size of a home. Webster defines luxury as "a condition of abundance or great ease and comfort. An indulgence. . .that provides pleasure, satisfaction, or ease."

Because it's not just about money or even square footage, luxury can be built into any home, from a tiny cottage to a hill-covering mansion. The goal of *DIY Projects for Luxurious Living* is to help you add details to your home—details that provide pleasure, satisfaction, or ease to help you create abundance. In today's environment where houses look practically the same from block to block, adding a touch of luxury is also a satisfying way to make your home stand out from the crowd.

The book is divided into chapters, each filled with information on a specific type of room or space: home gyms, home theaters, cigar lounges, libraries, wine cellars, home spas, and outdoor areas. Each chapter starts with a showcase of splendid examples meant to inspire and motivate you. Next, the All About section presents a collection of information and ideas you'll need to plan and design your projects effectively and efficiently. Finally, we feature actual projects with detailed photographs and step-by-step instructions to guide you through the process.

Inspiration

A paved courtyard and reflecting pool with a fountain adorn the grand entrance to this home.

The television has long served as an electronic fireplace around which we hear modern storytelling, and into today's luxury homes, flat panel televisions are often mounted prominently above the fireplace mantel.

A hoop in the driveway is enough for some, but more dedicated players may prefer a genuine home court like this enormous, high-ceilinged gym with its superior flooring, exceptional lighting, and all-weather comfort.

Size doesn't always equate with quality when it comes to home theaters. Consider the room layout, your intended primary use of the space, and your comfort when choosing which room to use for your home theater. Once you determine which space to use, you can accurately plan the layout and which products to use for the best overall experience.

Simple as 1-2-3: excellent lighting, great acoustics, and super-comfortable seating add up to a home theater that packs 'em in every night.

Home spas are all about high style, comfort, and convenience. Here a custom-built, tile soaking tub supports one end of a grand counter space. A vessel sink and wall-mounted faucet add panache to the simple setting.

Not for everyone, perhaps, but can you think of a bolder statement of luxury than a dedicated spa that does nothing but comfort tired feet?

Just a few unique features in your home can make a dramatic statement of luxury. The raised bowl sink and faucet has simple plumbing, but will draw attention from everyone who sees it.

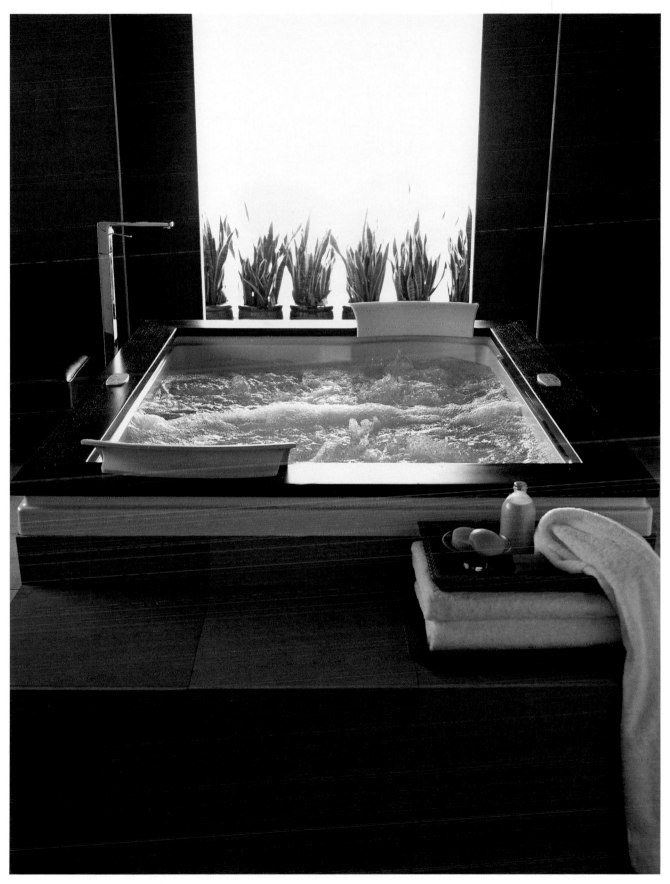

Stress melts away in the Zen-like atmosphere of this well-appointed home spa.

"Ladies and gentlemen: Shall we retire for cigars?" Such an invitation may conjure images of earlier, more genteel times, but with a lounge like this, it's as modern as today. Wood paneling, high ceilings, and leather furnishings make this cigar lounge as practical as it is elegant.

All apologies to Milton, paradise isn't lost. It can be found beneath the domed skylight of this grand library. With plenty of light and air, and bookcases on two levels, you can make yourself at home in luxury.

Floor to ceiling bookshelves combined with wainscot paneling are used here to create a delightful window seat reading alcove.

Wine cellars offer enthusiasts places to store, manage, and enjoy their collections. Here, a controlled environment preserves every precious drop, racking makes efficient use of space, and a tasting table provides entertainment space.

With sophisticated entertainment systems, a custom-built pool table, and bookcase-lined walls, this room delivers complete comfort as well as entertainment.

Glass block has many uses in modern up-scale homes and today's installation systems allow homeowners to easily work with it.

Home Gym Projects

There's no reason to fight traffic and bitter weather to get to the gym when getting to your workout could be as easy as walking down the hall or down the stairs. A home gym offers many advantages in addition to the easy commute: you always get to pick the music, there's no waiting for machines, and you'll have plenty of privacy in the showers.

Just think of it: you don't have to reset the seat in the weight cage or adjust the height of the chin-up bar. Everything is set up exactly the way you want it and ready whenever you are. All you have to do is slip into your favorite sweats and get to work.

A home gym is all about you and your preferences and interests. By tailoring the space to your own workouts, you can make the absolute most of every minute, in terms of results as well as in terms of good, old-fashioned fun.

Setting up a home gym is an easy, enjoyable project that can be accomplished in a weekend or two. In this chapter you'll find information on how to choose the location, how to provide adequate ventilation and good lighting, and how to choose equipment. We've also included instructions on how to create an inexpensive mirrored wall and install a ballet barre, a bar that supports you during stretching exercises.

In This Chapter:

- Gallery of Home Gyms
- All About Home Gyms
- Composite Wall Mirror
- Ballet Barre
- Chin-up Bar
- Rubber Roll Flooring

Gallery of Home Gyms

This breezy home gym has high ceilings, big windows, and fans to circulate the air. Good ventilation makes working out more comfortable and appealing.

What do a large, open space, rugged, low-nap carpet, good lighting, and a mirrored wall add up to? The setting for a home gym that's the envy of the entire neighborhood. With plenty of space around each piece of equipment, the whole family can work out

With its high ceilings, good lighting, and easy-to-clean flooring, this room was a natural for a home gym. Carefully placed mirrors multiply the room's ambient light and allow users to monitor their exercise form. Mats cushion the areas beneath the equipment and protect the flooring.

Shock-absorbent floor coverings, such as the cushioned tiles shown here, are an excellent choice for free-weight areas.

Large doors and windows provide exceptional ventilation for this home gym. Good ventilation prevents the build-up of mold and mildew in the naturally moist environment of a gym.

Bright, invigorating colors and large mirrors can help you get revved up for a workout, especially if the room's ambient light is limited.

All About Home Gyms

A home gym is more than a few pieces of little-used exercise equipment stashed in a vacant room. To make the leap to being an enjoyable workout room, your gym needs to be in a convenient, accessible space with good lighting, adequate ventilation, and comfortable flooring. It should have adequate electrical supply for a stereo and other entertainment components, as well as powered exercise equipment. It should be a pleasant space that's wisely outfitted to suit your needs.

A home gym can be fairly simple, but at a minimum you'll want a shock-absorbing floor and good light and ventilation. You'll also want to include custom details, such as mirrors or a ballet barre, that are related to your workout preferences.

Location

Look for space that's large enough to hold the equipment and filled with natural light and fresh air. Or, look for one that holds the possibility of adding plenty of light and adequate ventilation without too much difficulty. Avoid overly remote locations. If a home gym is tucked too far back in a corner, you may not be motivated to use it. Out of sight can mean out of mind, whereas walking past the open door to the gym can be a reminder to make the time to use it.

The basement is a popular location for home gyms, as is a guest bedroom. If you plan to build your gym in a basement, check the ceiling height. The ceiling should be at least 7 feet, but preferably 8 feet high to provide enough headroom for equipment and for stretching.

Unless circumstances—and your budget—allow for superior soundproofing, don't force the gym to share a common wall with an occupied bedroom. Working out can get pretty noisy, what with the clanking of weights, the pounding rhythm of music, or the television cranked up so it can be heard over the whir of the treadmill.

Space Requirements ▸

Choose a location large enough to accommodate the equipment you own or plan to include, with plenty of access so you can use it comfortably. Diagram your potential location and possible arrangements of your equipment. Here is a list of some basic equipment and the space required for each.

- Treadmills: 30 square ft.
- Single-station Gym: 35 square ft.
- Free Weights: 20 to 50 square ft.
- Bikes: 10 square ft.
- Rowing Machines: 20 square ft.
- Stair Climbers: 10 to 20 square ft.
- Ski Machines: 25 square ft.
- Multi-station Gym: 50 to 200 square ft.

Belonging to a health club is no reason not to build a home gym. According to a recent survey from the International Health, Racquet and Sports Association (IHRSA), 67% of people who go to health clubs also own exercise equipment that they use at home.

Lighting

A flattering lighting plan is an important part of a home gym. Good lighting makes everyone look better. Looking good takes you several steps toward feeling good, and, as we all know, feeling good makes it easier to take on the challenges of the world, including an exercise plan.

Low-voltage track lights are especially good options for a home gym because they generate pleasant, focusable light without producing as much heat as standard track lighting. It may be appropriate to include some overhead fluorescent lights, but don't limit your lighting plan to those fixtures. Add some incandescent side or uplights, too, to balance shadows and the color of the ambient light.

Mirrors are a good addition to a home gym. They enhance the available light in addition to letting you see and correct your form and posture.

Ventilation

If your home gym has operable windows, ventilation shouldn't be a big problem. If it doesn't, mechanical ventilation will make the space more comfortable and pleasant. Installing an exhaust fan on a wall or in the ceiling will help remove moisture and unpleasant odors from the air.

Select a fan sized to provide adequate ventilation for the gym's square footage. According to The Home Ventilating Institute, the air in rooms other than kitchens and bathrooms should be replaced at least six times per hour; the replacement rate recommended for a kitchen is 15 times an hour and 8 times an hour for bathrooms. These are, of course, minimums, and a home gym has unique ventilation needs. You might want to discuss the project with a heating/ventilation/ and air conditioning (HVAC) expert before selecting an exhaust fan.

If the ceiling is high enough to make it workable, a ceiling fan can be a good addition, too.

Tip ▸

A wall-mounted vent fan can be installed to provide ventilation to supplement operating windows and to provide four-season air movement.

Flooring

Home gym floors have to be comfortable, durable, and easy to clean. Hardwood floors have some of the necessary give and clean up beautifully, but they have a tendency to get scuffed, scratched, and damaged easily. Carpet offers a fairly forgiving and durable surface, but keeping it clean can be a challenge in a gym.

Resilient flooring is one of the best options for floor covering in a home gym. Rubber flooring (see page 30) is particularly appropriate in a home gym: it's easy on the knees, simple to clean, and tough enough to stand up to hard use.

If your floor covering is not ideal and changing it is not an option, place large rubber anti-fatigue mats (you can buy them at building centers as well as flooring stores) in critical areas.

Manage Receptacles & Cords ▸

Most larger pieces of workout equipment, such as treadmills and elliptical machines, require electricity. Because it is a safety hazard to have extension cords running all over the floor of your home gym, make sure you have a sufficient number of electrical receptacles in your gym room. If you do not have an outlet every 6 feet along all walls, upgrade your wiring circuit.

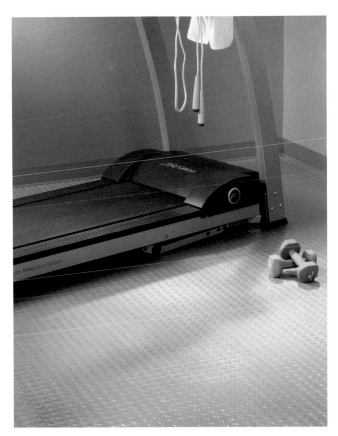

Gym flooring should be cushiony enough to be comfortable to lie on, while absorbing shocks and sound. Rubber flooring like this is an excellent choice. If you plan to do aerobics or dancing in the gym, you may prefer flooring that allows for sliding.

Entertainment Components

Whether it's a driving backbeat that keeps your feet moving or an upbeat tune that pumps you up, music makes working out easier and more fun for almost everyone. While some people do find music motivating, others consider it a distraction. Television and movies are the same: some people reward themselves for running on the treadmill or using the cross trainer by watching favorite programs while they work out. In most cases, there is no right or wrong—individual tastes vary and you simply need to identify and include components that motivate you personally. Weight lifting, however, requires careful attention from the aspect of safety as well as efficiency. Trainers suggest focusing on the specific muscles being used while lifting. Listening to music is unlikely to interfere with that focus, but television and movies might.

An entertainment center houses stereo and video components and offers storage space for CDs and your favorite workout DVDs.

Fitness Equipment ▶

Most experts agree that life's too short and time too precious to deal with cheap equipment. And, while it's often true that you get what you pay for, the most expensive products are not always the best. Research equipment online, consult retailers, and talk with fitness experts to determine what best meets your needs.

Populating a home gym is largely a matter of choosing equipment that can help you reach your goals. Some types of equipment help you build strength and muscle mass (resistance bands, weight machines, free weights); others help you improve cardiovascular fitness (treadmills, elliptical trainers, stationary bikes). Most of today's professional trainers recommend building core strength as well as doing cardiovascular and weight training.

Diagram the placement of the equipment you plan to include. Next, plan to place electrical outlets as necessary to serve not only the equipment you have but any you hope to add over time.

- Swiss (or Stability) balls ($20 to $40) help you improve core muscle strength, balance, and stability.
- Resistance bands ($10 to $20) come in different strengths, usually indicated by colors. These bands help you lengthen, strengthen, and tone your muscles.
- Balance trainers ($50 to $120), such as wobble boards and balance balls, help you develop core strength and balance that will prevent injuries.
- Medicine balls ($20 to $75) help you condition your abs and upper body.

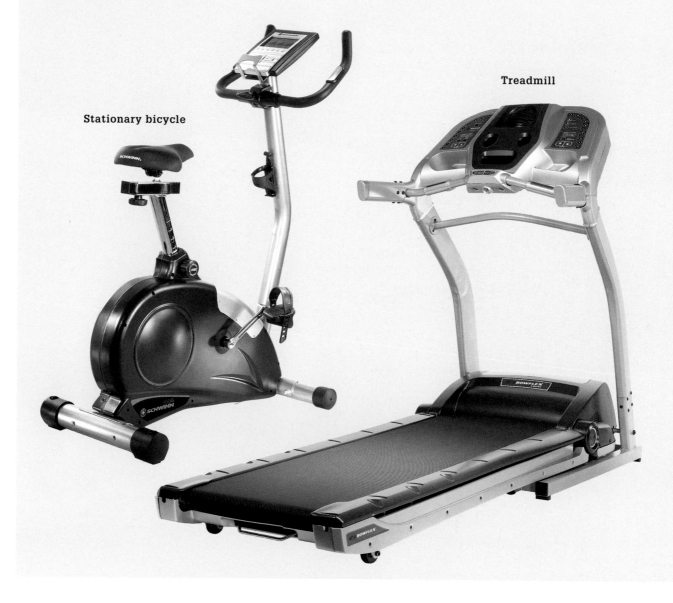

Stationary bicycle

Treadmill

- Free weights (about $1.00 a pound) can be used in exercises for the entire body.
- Weight benches ($100 to $500) can be fixed or adjustable and may or may not have racks to hold weights or bars. They help you get into position for a variety of lifts.
- Weight machines, also called single-station gyms, ($200 to $3,000 and up) provide stations and weights for strength training. Look for a unit that is designed to fit within the space you have available and one you can add accessories to as you progress in your training.
- Treadmills ($200 to $5,000 and up) come with every bell and whistle you can imagine and a few you probably can't. Whether or not you want a TV with DVD player built into the control panel is strictly a personal issue, but other features are easier to define. You want a unit that runs quietly. It needs to be designed to protect your knees by absorbing as much shock as possible, and the belt should be durable. The motor needs to be reliable and heavy enough to stand up to the weight of its users.
- Elliptical trainers ($500 to $4,000 and up) duplicate walking or running but without impact on your joints. The egg-shaped (elliptical) motion takes a little getting used to, but once you get the hang of it, it can be like walking on air. The arms let you work out your upper body along with your legs. Key features include a smooth motion and durable mechanisms.

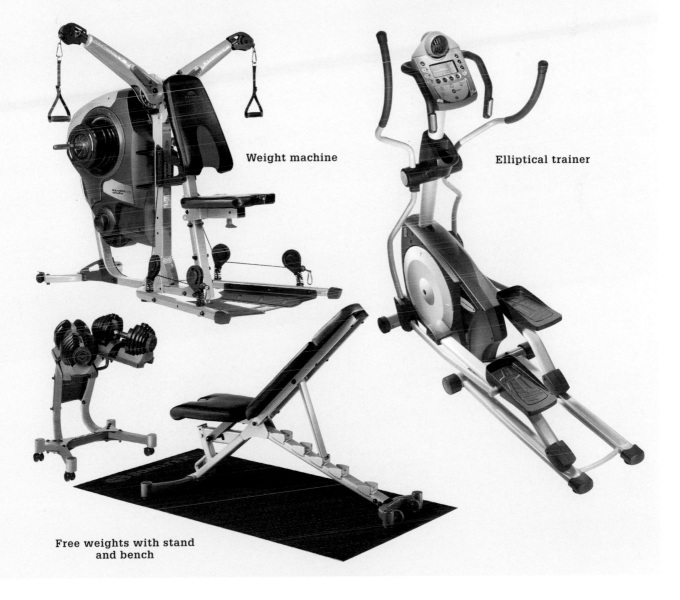

Weight machine

Elliptical trainer

Free weights with stand and bench

Composite Wall Mirror

Most of us have love/hate relationships with mirrors at the best of times, and few of us consider the moments we're dressed in workout clothes—especially spandex—to be the best of times. Even so, a mirrored wall is a valuable addition to a home gym. Mirrors let you observe your form during exercise and may even motivate you to keep pressing onward and upward. There's something about a mirrored wall that simply makes a room feel more like a gym.

Large plate-glass mirrors can be extremely expensive and require professional installation. Few do-it-yourselfers are prepared to handle mirrors wider than 4 feet. On the other hand, mirrored tiles are reasonably priced and simple to install, but the results—joints every 12 inches—can be disappointing.

Full-length, frameless mirrors are widely available at home centers, hardware stores, and glass centers. They offer views close to those of large plate-glass mirrors, but because they are thin and lightweight they are still easy for a do-it-yourselfer to handle. In this project, we hung three 16 × 60-inch frameless mirrors side-by-side to create the effect of a mirrored wall. Surrounded by a simple frame, this installation is an attractive alternative to a plate-glass mirror.

Hanging a series of inexpensive mirrors side by side creates a full-length mirror that works beautifully in a home gym.

Tools & Materials ▸

Stud finder	Mirror adhesive
Laser or carpenter's level	(3) 8' lengths of doorstop molding
Tape measure	Fine-grit sandpaper
Drill	Paint
Tack hammer	Paintbrush
(3) 16" × 60" frameless mirrors	Finish nails
Mirror J-clips	Wood filler

Tip ▸

Special mirror adhesive and J-clips are designed to hold mirrors securely without scratching the backing. You can find them at home centers, hardware stores, glass retailers, and on the Internet.

How to Install a Composite Mirror

Locate and mark the wall studs in the installation area, using an electronic stud finder. Measure and mark the position of the bottoms of the mirrors 8" above the floor. Create a level reference line at this height. Outline the project area. If necessary, adjust the position of the installation area to make sure that each mirror will cover at least one wall stud.

Locate and mark positions for J-clips centered over studs along the reference line marking the bottoms of the mirrors. Also mark clip positions at the tops of the mirrors. Clips are not installed at the sides of the mirrors.

Drill pilot holes and then drive screws through the J-clips to fasten them to the walls. Repeat to install clips for remaining mirrors. Spread mirror adhesive on the wall and set the mirror in place, resting on the J-clips. Let the adhesive dry according to manufacturer's directions.

Lightly sand the doorstop molding, then prime and paint it. When the paint is dry, measure the mirror installation and cut molding pieces to fit the perimeter of the mirror installation. Pieces should butt cleanly against the mirror edges. Tack the molding in place, using a tack hammer and finish nails. Fill the nail holes and touch up the paint.

Ballet Barre

A ballet barre (pronounced "bar") is a pole or two parallel poles attached horizontally to a wall. Dancers, especially ballet dancers, use barres to support themselves during warm-up routines, but you don't have to be a dancer to use one. Anyone who does stretching routines or strengthening exercises will find a barre useful in their home gym.

The best barres are sturdy, stable, smooth bars positioned at a comfortable height for the user. Traditionally, barres are wood rods supported by (but spinning freely in) metal brackets attached to the wall or floor. They may include one or two poles, depending on the needs of the user and the number of users.

Barres are typically positioned between 40 and 46 inches from the floor. One of the great luxuries of installing your own is that you can put it at any height you wish. Step 2 of the project describes determining the ideal height for you. The measurement from step 2 (page 27) is the ideal height for a single barre. If you're installing a double barre, position the top barre at this height.

The height of the lower barre will be determined by the configuration of the bracket.

It is critical that the barre be properly supported. Make sure the brackets are anchored into wall studs and positioned to fully support your weight on the barre. In this project, we describe the installation of an 8-foot barre. If yours is longer or shorter, adjust the positions of the brackets accordingly.

Tools & Materials ›

Stud finder
Laser or
    carpenter's level
Tape measure
Drill
Single or double
    ballet barre brackets
    (at least 2)

Two 1¼" wood
    poles, 8' long
    (preferably
    hardwood, such
    as oak or maple)
Fine-grit sandpaper
Paintbrushes
Polyurethane finish

A **ballet barre** provides support for a wide variety of stretches and exercises, many of which are common warm-ups for dancers.

How to Install a Ballet Barre

Sand the barres until the surfaces are absolutely smooth to the touch. If desired, apply stain and let them dry. Apply several thin coats of polyurethane finish to each, allowing the finish to dry between coats. *Tip: Drive an 8d finish nail partway into each end and rest the head of each nail on a sawhorse to support the rod.*

Shopping Tip ▸

Brackets for ballet barres are widely available from suppliers of dance accessories and online (search for "ballet barre brackets"). When shopping, compare materials and spacing requirements as well as prices. Check the maximum span between brackets, the maximum overhang, and the size of barre the brackets will accommodate.

Determine the ideal height for the barre by taking measurements from the user. Have the user stand with his or her back straight and feet together and flat on the floor. Relax the shoulders and bend the elbows up until the forearms and hands are parallel with the floor. Bend the elbow down until the fingertips drop by one inch. Measure from the fingertips to the floor to find the ideal barre height.

Locate and mark the wall studs in the installation area, using an electronic stud finder. Measure and mark the height for the top barre, as determined in step 2. Create a level reference line at this height.

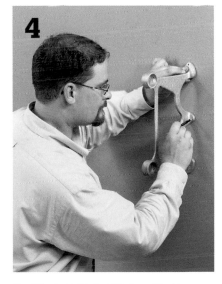

Position each bracket so the top of the barre opening is even with the reference line (the top of the bracket likely will not align with the line). Center the bracket on the wall stud marks, and trace the locations of the screw holes in each bracket onto the wall with a pencil. For a 96" barre, the brackets should be approximately 64" apart.

(continued)

Measure down from the screw marks to the floor and compare the measurements to make sure the brackets will be parallel to the floor. Adjust as necessary until the measurements are identical for each bracket.

Drill a pilot hole for each screw, centered in the screw hole location marks.

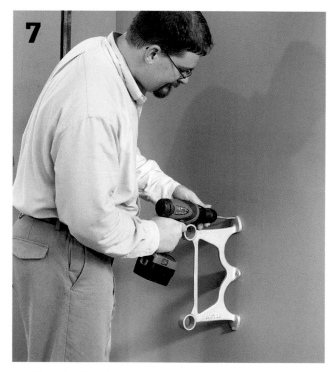

Position the first bracket and drive screws at the screw locations to secure it to the wall. Repeat with the second bracket. Take care not to overdrive the screws, as this can cause the screw heads to break off. *Note: If the wall is less than 14-ft. long, install barres now (before screwing second bracket to the wall).*

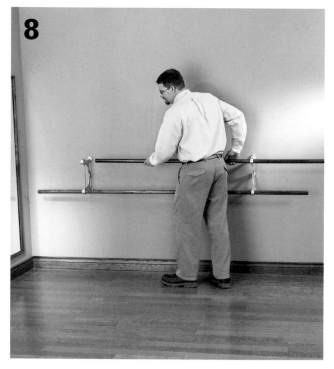

Insert one barre into the lower brackets and a second into the upper brackets. Position each barre so it projects approximately 16" from the brackets on each end. The rods should fit loosely enough in the brackets that they can spin freely.

Chin-up Bar

Sometimes the most useful items are the simplest. Take the classic chin-up bar. A fixture in many homes a couple of generations before the creation of phrases like "step aerobics" or "elliptical trainer," the humble chin-up bar is inconspicuous when not in use, but is always ready to go when you feel a need for an upper body workout.

Chin-up bars that are mounted in a doorway are inexpensive and easy to install; they literally consume zero floorspace. More elaborate models are wall-mounted, with brackets that project the bar out into the room—in some cases, far enough to allow you to hang from your knees.

On this page you'll see just how easy it is to install a chin-up bar that mounts in a doorway and costs approximately $20.

Most doorway chin-up bars fit over round brackets that are screwed to the tops of your door jambs. Measure down 1½" from the head jamb on each side of the doorway, and mark reference lines. Butt a bracket up against the line and mark drilling points for the screw holes. Make sure the brackets are the same distance from the edge of the jamb. Attach the brackets with #8 × 2½" wood screws (these should be long enough to penetrate into the studs of the door's rough opening).

The chin-up bar itself spins and telescopes in much the same way as a shower curtain rod. Adjust the bar so it fits between the brackets, and then slip one end over the bracket (there may be a set screw to tighten). Then, spin the bar to extend it until the other end is fully seated against the other bracket. Test the bar from time to time to make sure it is not retracting and becoming shorter.

Rubber Roll Flooring

Once a mark of restaurants and retailers, sheet rubber flooring has become an option for homeowners as well. It's resilient, durable, and stable, holding up well under the heaviest and most demanding use. Better still, it's comfortable to walk on and easy to maintain.

The durability and resilience of rubber provide benefits in two ways. First, the flooring takes just about any kind of use without showing damage. Second, it absorbs shock in proportion to its thickness. Heavier rubber floors help prevent fatigue, making them comfortable for standing, walking, and even strenuous exercise.

Many new flooring products are made from recycled rubber, which saves landfill space and reduces the consumption of new raw materials. This is one place a petroleum-based product is environmentally friendly.

To install rubber sheet flooring on top of wood, use only exterior-grade plywood, one side sanded. Do not use lauan plywood, particleboard, chipboard, or hardboard. Make sure the surface is level, smooth, and securely fastened to the subfloor.

Tools & Materials ▸

Adhesive
Chalk line
Cleaning supplies
Utility knife
Flat-edged trowel
Measuring tape

Mineral spirits
Notched trowel
Painter's tape
Straightedge
Weighted roller

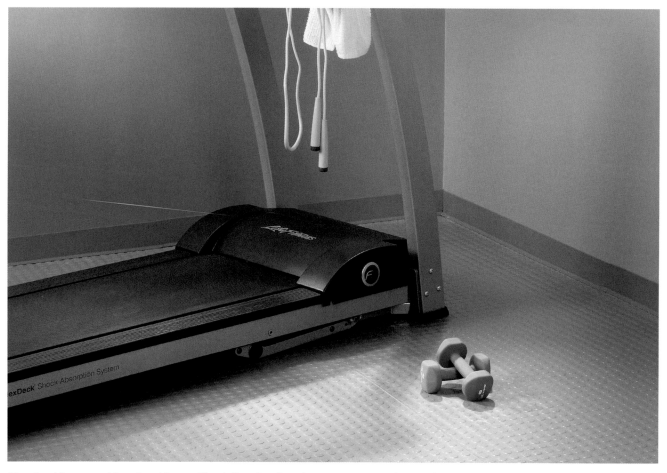

Sheet rubber provides durable, resilient flooring for a home gym. It stands up to hard use, absorbs shock, and cleans up easily.

How to Install Rubber Roll Floorcovering

Mark the first strip of rubber roll flooring for cutting to length. Start on the longest wall, and mark the cutting line so the strip will be a couple of inches too long. Use a straightedge guide to mark the cutting lines, and then cut with a sharp utility knife (be sure to put a backer board under the material before cutting it).

Set the first strip against the long wall so the overage in length is equal at each end. Cut the next strip to length and then butt it up against the first strip. Adjust the second strip so it overlaps the first strip by 1 to 1½ inches, making sure the strips remain parallel. Lay out all of the strips in the room in this manner.

Cut the strips to create perfectly matched seams. With a backer board underneath the seam, center a straightedge on the top strip and carefully cut through both strips in the overlap area. Change utility knife blades frequently, and don't try to make the cut in one pass unless your flooring is very thin.

Remove the waste material from the seam area and test the fit of the strips. Because they were cut together, they should align perfectly. Make sure you don't adjust the position of one of the strips or the seams may not align properly.

(continued)

Fold back one half of the first strip so half of the flooring subbase is exposed. Again, take care not to shift the position of the flooring strip.

Apply the adhesive recommended by the flooring manufacturer to the exposed floor, using a notched trowel. Avoid getting adhesive on the surface of the flooring, and make sure the adhesive is applied all the way up to the walls and just past the seam area.

Lower the roll slowly onto the adhesive, making sure not to allow any air to become trapped underneath. Never leave adhesive ridges or puddles; they will become visible on the surface.

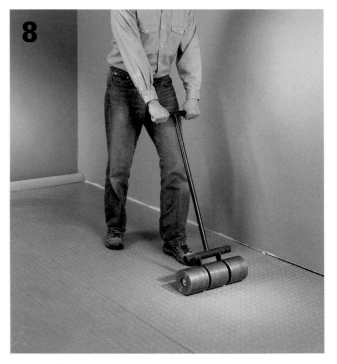

Roll the floor immediately with a 100-pound roller to squeeze out any trapped air and maximize contact between the roll and the adhesive. With each pass of the roller, overlap the previous pass by half. Roll the width first, then the length, and re-roll after 30 minutes.

Fold back the second half of the first roll and the first half of the second roll. Apply and spread the adhesive as before. Spread the adhesive at a 90° angle to the seams. This will reduce the chance of having adhesive squeeze up through the seams. Continue installing strips in this manner.

Clean up adhesive squeezeout or spills immediately using a rag and mineral spirits. At seams, take care not to allow mineral spirits to get underneath the flooring, as it will ruin the adhesive.

Press down on any bubbles or on seams that do not have a seamless appearance. If a seam resists lying flat, set a board and weights over it overnight. It is a good idea to hand-roll all seams with a J-roller, in addition to rolling the entire floor with a floor roller.

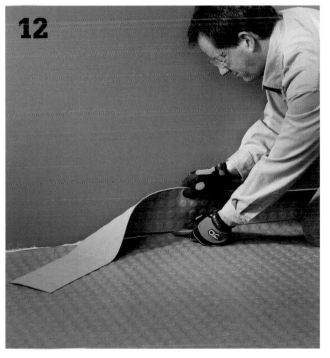

Trim off excess flooring at the ends using a utility knife. Leaving a slight gap between the flooring and the wall is fine as long as you plan to install base molding.

Home Theater Projects

Big screen? Check. Outstanding sound system? Check. Stadium seating? Check. Great goodies? Check.

If you think this could only be describing a typical trip to the local multiplex, you're wrong. It could be a private theater in your very own home, open any hour of the day or night. Here, you've always got the best seat in the house, and your favorite beverages are on hand.

When it comes to your home theater, think big screens, surround sound, and great acoustics. Think technology and media storage. Think comfort and variety. Creating a home theater is more than a weekend project—it requires a substantial investment of both time and money. This chapter provides information and projects that will help you understand the issues at hand and take steps to make sure your home theater is the absolute best it can be within your space and budget. From superior soundproofing to meeting the electrical demands of the equipment to placement of the equipment and furniture, you'll find it all right here.

In This Chapter:

- Gallery of Home Theaters
- All About Home Theaters
- Soundproofing a Home Theater
- Routing Cables & Wires
- Installing an Audio System
- Installing Acoustic Ceiling Tile
- Building Media Display Storage
- DIY Projection Theater

Gallery of Home Theaters

Risers built into the floor to elevate the rows of seats give everyone an unobstructed view of the screen.

Glare ruins a viewing experience. In rooms with windows, install heavy drapes to darken the room when necessary.

If drama is your style, make your theater as entertaining as the movies you watch! Choose a theme and collect furnishings and accessories that play the role to the hilt.

The focus is all on fun in this entertainment area. With the components tucked into a wall niche, the wide screen positioned above a bank of cabinets, and the projector hanging from the high ceiling, the working elements of the theater take a back seat.

Choose a screen that delivers the impact you're looking for. The action drives straight at you with a super-sized screen like this one.

This theater incorporates traditional furniture to evoke the feeling of a living room in a dedicated theater.

Large rooms can accommodate large screens without being overwhelmed by them. This home theater offers a superior viewing experience along with excellent sound in a simple, contemporary setting.

All About Home Theaters

With rapid advances in audio and video equipment and networking possibilities, more and more of today's homeowners are investing in dedicated rooms to enjoy and share their music, movies, favorite TV shows, or computer games. If you are one of them, you want a comfortable, attractive space for relaxing and for maximizing your audio/visual experiences.

In order to provide the kind of experience serious enthusiasts are looking for, a home theater must blend technology with design, while folding the equipment into the decor in a way that enhances both. To create a successful home entertainment room, you need to consider room selection and design, equipment, and furnishings just to get started.

Because they are slim and can be hung on a wall, modern flat-panel televisions let you create a home theater of sorts in practically any room in your house. If your theater will be doing double duty, try and pick an activity that is entertainment related, such as a game room.

Room Selection and Layout

Choosing an appropriate space makes it easier to get the results you want. Here are some things to keep in mind:

- An enclosed, rectangular room offers the best acoustics.
- Bare surfaces create harsh sound levels. This means, for example, that carpeting is a better flooring choice than hardwood.
- Vaulted ceilings are not ideal. They make it difficult to achieve excellent sound.
- The less ambient (natural) light the room has, the easier it is to control the lighting.

Reduce Collateral Noise ▸

Sound is vibration, and at high levels vibration causes rattles. To tame rattles:

- Tighten mechanical connections on all fixtures.
- Strap down or insulate plumbing pipes.
- Wrap baffles around air ducts.
- Cushion edges of heat registers with self-adhesive foam tape.
- Put rubber bumpers on the backs of picture frames.

One way to reduce collateral noise like rattling is to attach self-adhesive bumpers to the backs of picture frames so they don't clatter against the wall when your audio is cranked up.

(continued)

Setting up a home theater requires attention to details. From the positions of screens and speakers to the best type of draperies, every detail plays an important role in creating the best possible experience.

The best place to start organizing your entertainment room is with the video display (television) and the seating. The arrangement of other components, such as speakers, flows from the placement of these first, most basic elements of the room.

Experts differ on the best distance from a screen to the seating areas. If you're confused, you may want to consult a designer or even your equipment retailer. One respected resource, The Society of Motion Picture and Television Engineers (SMPTE) recommends at least a 30-degree field of view from the seats farthest from the screen to optimize picture quality and reduce eye strain for those watching.

Free viewing distance calculators are available at many internet sites. In most cases, you simply indicate the size and shape (square or rectangle) of the screen and the calculator responds with the ideal viewing distance.

You'll get the best sound if the seating areas are centered between the surround speakers. Position front speakers, high-frequency drivers, or tweeters at seated ear level. Position the surrounds slightly above seated ear level. Experiment with the placement of the subwoofer. (Bass sound is nondirectional, so there are no specific rules.)

Placing speakers close to the intersection of two room surfaces (two walls, a wall and the ceiling, or a wall and the floor) strengthens the bass output; moving speakers away from these intersections reduces bass output.

It's best not to put the video screen opposite a bank of windows if at all possible. If you can't avoid this, cover the windows with draperies lined with blackout fabric to control the light. If there are windows in the room, even if they're not opposite the screen, choose lined draperies over blinds, which can interfere with sound quality.

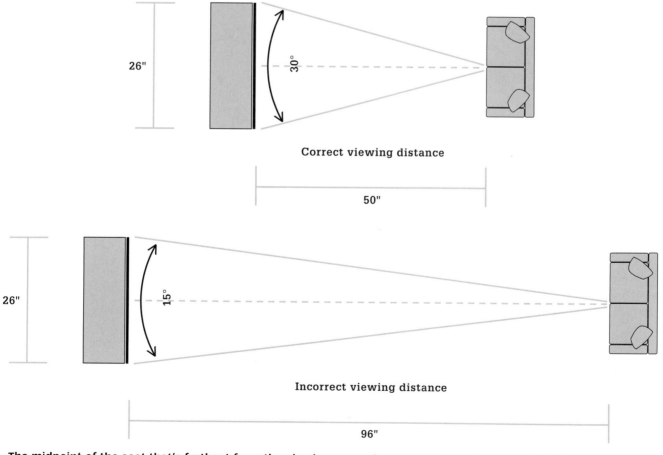

Correct viewing distance

50"

Incorrect viewing distance

96"

The midpoint of the seat that's furthest from the viewing screen in your theater should create a field-of-view angle of 30° when triangulated with the sides of the viewing screen, as seen here.

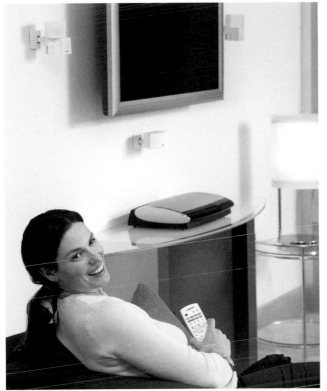

Front speakers, high-frequency drivers, and tweeters in your surround sound system should be positioned so they are around ear level when listeners are seated.

The ideal home theater room is windowless, but if your room features windows, especially with direct sun exposure, cover them with lined draperies. For the ultimate in light blocking and sound deadening, choose acoustical blackout drapes like those seen here.

Equipment

More than any other component, audio and visual equipment defines the success or failure of your home theater. Technology in these areas advances very quickly and keeping up with state-of-the art stuff is a never-ending process. You can subscribe to magazines dedicated to nothing but video and stereo equipment. We've done our best here to provide some useful information that's current as of this book's copyright date, however. See "Choosing & Using Audio/Visual Equipment," pages 46 to 49.

If your home theater has another function, such as a living room, a system of floor-to-ceiling cabinets can be employed to keep components out of sight during tea time.

Furnishings

When evaluating cabinets or storage/display options, remember that you'll need access to your components and cables from time to time. Remember, too, that each component has a heat vent and that these vents need open space to dissipate heat and protect your equipment. Entertainment center-type cabinets are popular, but open shelves provide both access and plenty of vent space.

If staying on the leading edge of technology is important to you, it's probable that you'll be changing equipment and moving components from time to time. Selecting modular furnishings or pieces that can be used in a variety of ways makes these changes easier and less expensive over time.

Theater-style seating is a popular option for home entertainment rooms, but a choice you should consider carefully. The pieces tend to be quite large and can tie you to one particular room arrangement. Other, smaller seating pieces may be more adaptable to your changing needs.

Soft furnishings and window coverings improve the sound quality and help contain the sound to the room as well.

Traditional, dedicated theater seats are not meant to be moved around. Upholstered in washable leather, these heavy-duty reclining seats feature cupholders and broad arm rests.

Choosing & Using Audio/Visual Equipment ▸

Although you do have quite a bit of choice in your equipment purchases based on budget, lifestyle, and personal taste, the nuts and bolts of all systems are similar. They include the video display, the signal source, the audio and visual signal source equipment, and a piece of equipment to process it all—often a receiver. When the lights go down in your home theater, the quality and compatibility of these parts that make up the systemic whole will define the nature of your watching and listening experiences.

Selecting the audio and visual equipment that's best for your home entertainment room doesn't require that you become completely immersed in the high-tech A/V world, but a little planning up front will help you make some good decisions.

PICTURE-PERFECT: THE VIDEO DISPLAY

The question of which is more important, audio or video, is hotly debated among home theater enthusiasts. Some desire the all-consuming impact of a powerful explosion coming at them in surround sound; others appreciate the crispness and color accuracy of properly calibrated video images. Either way, one thing is certain: The video screen plays an extremely important role in the overall entertainment experience. After all, where would theater be without the act of viewing something, whether it's a live Shakespearean troupe performing *Romeo and Juliet* or the latest blockbuster movie being projected onto a video screen. When choosing a video display, consider what size and type are best for your needs.

Despite the recent trend of downsizing gear in the home theater marketplace—with the proliferation of bookshelf or "lifestyle" speakers and emaciated components—bigger is usually better when it comes to video. That isn't to say you can't find video screens, such as plasmas, with a small footprint and slim profile, but the surface area of the screen should be reasonably expansive. Screens, whether television screens or screens used with projectors (also known as projection screens), are measured diagonally. This diagonal measurement stems from the 1980s, when marketers realized that the biggest linear dimension of a rectangle is its diagonal measurement; advertising on this measurement made screens seem bigger. Choose as big a screen as you can, keeping in mind both the proportions of your living space and optimal viewing distances.

When you're pondering television and screen sizes, keep these points in mind: Normally, televisions larger than 60" have their own built-in stand (their weight prohibits them from resting safely on separate TV stands). They tend to be hard to move and they consume lots of floorspace. Some people build custom cabinetry around floorstanding models to minimize their cumbersome appearance.

Most sets smaller than 60" can be placed on a TV rack or other furniture that is strong enough to support its weight. Choose furniture to match the style of your room. For example, pick a sleek wire rack with frosted glass if your room is contemporary or minimalist in style; go for wood A/V furniture for a warmer, rustic look; or pick out funky, bright pieces to liven up a room.

VIDEO RULE OF THUMB

Projection systems—a separate projector and screen—require precise placement at a fixed distance from the video screen. This makes them good options for a dedicated home theater, which offers more placement options than a multipurpose room. Rear-projection televisions, which are 36" and larger, are good for big media rooms, and direct-view televisions, which tend to be 36" and under, are better suited for smaller rooms.

Just because your TV set is large doesn't mean it has to stick out like a sore thumb. This rear-projection television is surprisingly svelte, and the red accents on its back are picked up elsewhere in the room.

(continued)

SOUND ADVICE: WHAT YOU NEED TO KNOW ABOUT SPEAKERS

Imagine sitting on the edge of a river. In front of you is the sound of the river crashing around rocks; behind you, the sound of feet on damp earth as someone approaches. Above, the sound of birds chirping filters through the trees. We live in a three-dimensional world, but reproducing its 3-D soundfield in the two-dimensional world of motion pictures is not easy. To accomplish this auditory trick, a basic audio setup consists of no fewer than five speakers, plus a subwoofer, arranged more or less symmetrically around the audience. Discrete sound from a soundtrack, unique to each speaker, is channeled, or distributed, to the five speakers and the subwoofer, so you'll often hear industry buffs referring to 5.1 channels of audio when referring to a 5.1 surround speaker system. Channels, simply, are the surround sound information going to the speaker, not the speaker itself. It is a slight distinction, but one that can save you a headache as you learn more.

Put the center speaker as close to the video image as possible. Make sure it is magnetically shielded so it doesn't interfere with the picture or damage any VHS tapes in the vicinity. Don't use your TV's speaker as a

Speakers don't have to be eyesores in an otherwise blemish-free room. In fact, many speakers come in various finishes, such as cherrywood and glossy black, so you can incorporate them easily into the design of your room. Here, the light wood Infinity speakers are as much a design statement as the hardwood floors and big, airy windows.

center channel or use mismatched speakers (especially for the front left and right and center speakers). Buying speakers as a sonically matched set ensures they have the same capabilities and sonic characteristics, which in turn will give you smooth, even sound.

Don't put speakers in corners. The sound will bounce off the walls, ceiling, and floor, producing reverberation and sonic reflections. Your main speakers should be several feet from the corners of the room. Avoid putting speakers inside cabinets. Instead, use speaker stands or mount small speakers on walls.

SIGNAL SOURCES

Sources are the soul of home theater. Without them we would have nothing to watch, nothing to listen to, nothing to keep us entertained. DVD players, VCRs, laserdisc players, CD players, digital video recorders, satellite television, and even cable television all pump the stuff we want to see and hear into our systems. Tailor your sources to your own desires. If music is not important to you, focus on video. You can, for example, use your DVD player as a CD player, eliminating the need to buy a separate CD transport.

On the other hand, if music is your main interest, put more time and money into perfecting your system's audio portion. In this case, you might spend your money on a 500-disc CD jukebox or a Super-Audio CD/DVD-Audio (SACD/DVD–audio) universal player to play your collection of high-resolution audio on rather than a costly projector and high-end DVD player that would just collect dust.

Because it processes all of the sound and video information, the receiver is the brain in your home theater. It comes with a gaggle of inputs and outputs on its rear panel that lets you connect your speakers, your sources, your video display, and so on, and allows them to communicate with one another. A receiver also decodes soundtracks from surround-sound-formatted source material, such as a DVD's Dolby Digital 5.1 soundtrack. Then it takes surround effects and delivers them to the appropriate channel, or speaker. A receiver provides power, measured in watts, to every speaker in your system. Switching is also handled by this jack-of-all-trades. Switching allows you to change from one source to another, such as a DVD player to satellite television, without having to shuffle plugs into your TV, which can accept no more than one or two sources at a time.

When shopping for a receiver, look for one that has the surround sound decoding capabilities you require. That is, if you plan to listen to 5.1 home theater, make sure your receiver is Dolby Digital– and DTS–capable. Also, be sure the receiver has all the inputs and outputs you need. For example, if your TV has a component video output, buy a receiver with a component video input. Most midpriced receivers have one of everything, but it pays to double-check.

Pages 46 to 49 excerpted from Home Theater Design *by Krissy Rushing.*

You might not recognize it, but this small black box mounted to the wall is actually a state-of-the-art receiver and transmitter that is linked wirelessly to additional signal sources as well as to the speakers.

Soundproofing a Home Theater

Good soundproofing is vital to a luxurious entertainment room. Music and movies are best enjoyed when they don't have to compete with noise from other rooms or from the outside world. By the same token, people in the rest of the house should not be forced to listen to music or soundtracks from the entertainment room.

Sound is created by vibrations traveling through air. Consequently, the best ways to reduce sound transmission are by limiting airflow and blocking or absorbing vibrations. Effective soundproofing typically involves a combination of methods.

Stopping airflow—through walls, ceilings, floors, windows, and doors—is essential to any soundproofing effort. (Even a 2-foot-thick brick wall would not be very soundproof if it had cracks in the mortar.) It's also the simplest way to make minor improvements. Because you're dealing with air, this kind of soundproofing is a lot like weatherizing your home: add weatherstripping and door sweeps, seal air leaks with caulk, install storm doors and windows, etc. The same techniques that keep out the cold also block exterior noise and prevent sound from traveling between rooms.

After reducing airflow, the next level of soundproofing is to improve the sound-blocking qualities of your walls and ceilings. Engineers rate soundproofing performance of wall and ceiling assemblies using a system called Sound Transmission Class, or STC. The higher the STC rating, the more sound is blocked by the assembly. For example, if a wall is rated at 30 to 35 STC, loud speech can be understood through the wall. At 42 STC, loud speech is reduced to a murmur. At 50 STC, loud speech cannot be heard through the wall.

Standard construction methods typically result in a 28 to 32 STC rating, while soundproofed walls and ceilings can carry ratings near 50. To give you an idea of how much soundproofing you need, a sleeping room at 40 to 50 STC is quiet enough for most people; a reading room is comfortable at 35 to 40 STC. For another gauge, consider the fact that increasing the STC rating of an assembly by 10 reduces the perceived sound levels by 50 percent. The chart on page 45 lists the STC ratings of several wall and ceiling assemblies.

Improvements to walls and ceilings usually involve increasing the mass, absorbancy, or resiliency of the assembly; often, a combination is best. Adding layers of drywall increases mass, helping a wall resist the vibrational force of sound (⅝" fire-resistant drywall works best because of its greater weight and density). Insulation and soundproofing board absorb sound. Soundproofing board is available through drywall suppliers and manufacturers. Some board products are gypsum-based; others are lightweight fiberboard. Installing resilient steel channels over the framing or old surface and adding a new layer of drywall increases mass, while the channels allow the surface to move slightly and absorb vibrations. New walls built with staggered studs and insulation are highly effective at reducing vibration.

In addition to these permanent improvements, you can reduce noise by decorating with soft materials that absorb sound. Rugs and carpet, drapery, fabric wall hangings, and soft furniture help reduce atmospheric noise within a room. Acoustical ceiling tiles effectively absorb and help contain sound within a room but do little to prevent sound from entering the room.

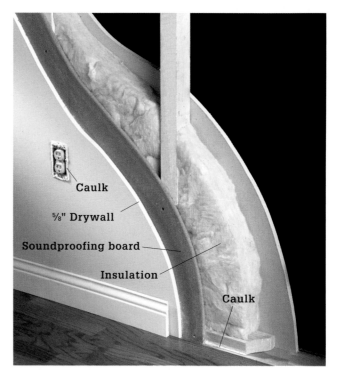

Adding soundproofing board and insulation are among the many simple ways you can reduce noise in your home.

STC Ratings for Various Wall & Ceiling Constructions* ▸

Assembly	STC Rating
Wood-frame Walls	
2 × 4 wall; ½" drywall on both sides; no caulk	30
2 × 4 wall; ½" drywall on both sides; caulked	35
2 × 4 wall; ½" drywall on both sides; additional layer of ⅝" fire-resistant drywall on one side	38
2 × 4 wall; ½" drywall on both sides; additional layer of ⅝" fire-resistant drywall on both sides	40
2 × 4 wall; ½" drywall on both sides; insulated	39
Staggered-stud 2 × 4 wall; ⅝" fire-resistant drywall on each side; insulated	50
2 × 4 wall, soundproofing board (base layer) and ⅝" fire-resistant drywall on each side; insulated	50
2 × 4 wall with resilient steel channels on one side; ⅝" fire-resistant drywall on both sides; insulated	52
Steel-frame Walls	
3⅝" metal studs, spaced 24" on-center; ⅝" fire-resistant drywall on both sides	40
3⅝" metal studs, spaced 24" on-center, ½" fire-resistant drywall single layer on one side, doubled on other side; insulated	48
2½" metal studs, spaced 24" on-center; soundproofing board (base layer) and ½" fire-resistant drywall on both sides; insulated	50
Wood-frame Floor/Ceiling	
Drywall below; subfloor and resilient (vinyl) flooring above	32
⅝" fire-resistant drywall attached to resilient steel channels below; subfloor, pad, and carpet above	48
Double layer ⅝" fire-resistant drywall attached to resilient steel channels below; subfloor, pad, and carpet above	Up to 60

*All assemblies are sealed with caulk, except where noted. Ratings are approximate.

Tips for Reducing Exterior Noise ▸

Install weatherstripping on doors and windows to seal off any air leaks. If the wall framing around the door or window is exposed, make sure all cavities are filled with loosely packed insulation.

Add storm doors and windows to minimize air leaks and create an additional sound barrier. Use high-performance (airtight) storm units and maintain a 2" air gap between the storm and the primary unit.

Seal around pipes, A/C service lines, vents, and other penetrations in exterior walls, using expanding foam or caulk. Make sure through-wall A/C units are well-sealed along their perimeters.

Tips for Reducing Interior Noise ▶

Stop airflow between rooms by sealing the joints where walls meet floors. With finished walls, remove the shoe molding and spray insulating foam, acoustic sealant, or non-hardening caulk under the baseboards. Also seal around door casings. With new walls, seal along the top and bottom plates.

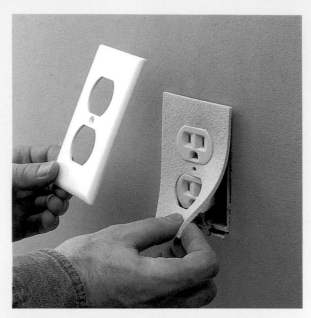

Cover switch and receptacle boxes with foam gaskets to prevent air leaks. Otherwise, seal around the box perimeter with acoustic sealant or caulk and seal around the knockout where the cables enter the box.

Seal the edges of the doorframe with closed cell foam tape and install a rubber door sweep at the bottom (see pages 86 to 87). Cut self-adhesive soundproof mat (see Resources) to fit the surface of the door and install it. Cover the mat with fabric that complements the décor of the room.

Reduce sound transmission through ductwork by lining ducts with special insulation. If a duct supplying a quiet room has a takeoff point close to that of a noisy room, move one or both ducts so their takeoff points are as distant from each other as possible.

How to Install Resilient Steel Channels

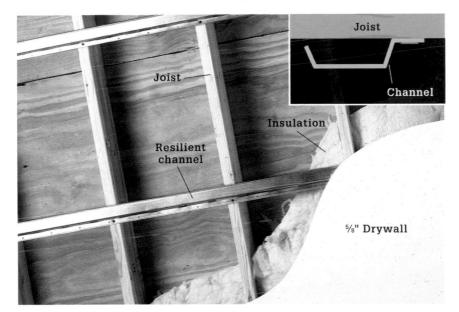

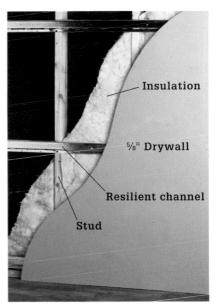

On ceilings, install channels perpendicular to the joists, spaced 24" on-center. Fasten at each joist with 1¼" type W drywall screws, driven through the channel flange. Stop the channels 1" short of all walls. Join pieces on long runs by overlapping the ends and fastening through both pieces. Insulate the joist bays with R-11 unfaced fiberglass or other insulation and install ⅝" fire-resistant drywall, run perpendicular to the channels. For double-layer application, install the second layer of drywall perpendicular to the first.

On walls, use the same installation techniques as with the ceiling application, installing the channels horizontally. Position the bottom channel 2" from the floor and the top channel within 6" of the ceiling. Insulate the stud cavities and install the drywall vertically.

How to Build Staggered-stud Partition Walls

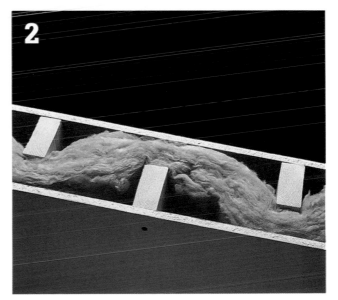

Frame new partition walls using 2 × 6 plates. Space the studs 12" apart, staggering them so alternate studs are aligned with opposite sides of the plates. Seal under and above the plates with acoustic sealant.

Weave R-11 unfaced fiberglass blanket insulation horizontally between the studs. Cover each side with one or more layers of ⅝" fire-resistant drywall.

Soundproofing Home Theaters

The walls of the average house are not designed to contain extreme sound levels. To combat this issue, there are numerous soundproofing products and materials available to help keep those on both sides of a home theater wall happy.

As discussed on page 50, engineers rate the soundproofing performance of wall and ceiling assemblies using a system called Sound Transmission Class (STC). Standard partition walls carry STC ratings of 28 to 32. Determining an appropriate STC rating for your home theater is dependent on a number of factors, such as the power of your multimedia system and the type of room opposite the wall, but a minimum of 60 STC is adequate for most. Remember: The higher the STC rating, the more sound is blocked.

But blocking sound is not the only consideration. The low frequencies generated by subwoofers cause vibrations, which in turn create unwanted noise within the room. The most effective approach for soundproofing a home theater is to install both sound barriers to minimize sound escaping and sound absorbers to reduce noise within the room.

Adding mass to walls and ceilings is an effective way to block sound. In new construction, staggered-stud partitions (page 53) or double stud partitions (two adjacent rows of studs) are possibilities. Hanging soundproofing board, sound-rated wallboard,

or multiple layers of wallboard can increase STC ratings significantly. Two of the most effective systems are resilient channels (page 53) and mass loaded vinyl (MLV) underlayment, a heavy vinyl sheeting that many manufacturers claim can more than double a wall's STC rating.

For sound absorption, closed-cell acoustical foam matting can be used to insulate between wallboard panels and framing. Similarly, padded tape minimizes transmission of sound vibration between wall panels and framing and can be used to line resilient channels for added insulation. Sound isolation mounting clips contain molded neoprene to provide added insulation between resilient channels and framing. Vibration pads made of cork and closed-cell acoustical foam or neoprene isolates sound vibration to reduce transmission between objects.

When fastening soundproofing and wallboard panels to resilient channels, leave ¼" between all panels at corners, and fill the gaps with acoustical caulk. All gaps, seams, and cracks should be filled with acoustical caulk. The more airtight a home theater, the more soundproof it is.

Whichever soundproofing products or materials you choose, make sure to follow the manufacturer's installation instructions to achieve the optimal performance.

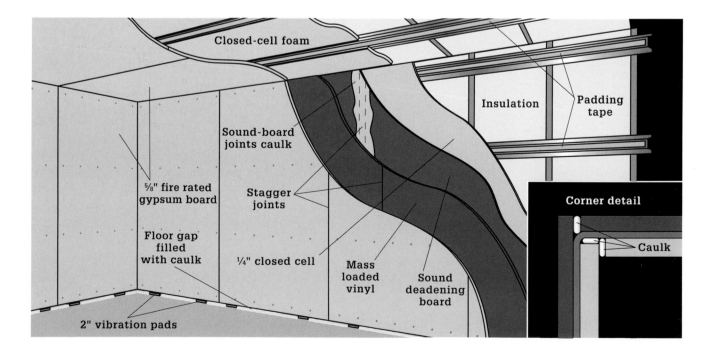

Tips for Soundproofing a Home Theater ▸

Use contact cement to glue ¼" closed-cell acoustical matting directly to existing wall and ceiling surfaces or to the backside of wallboard panels in new construction.

Apply self-adhesive padded tape to resilient channels or directly to the edges of framing members.

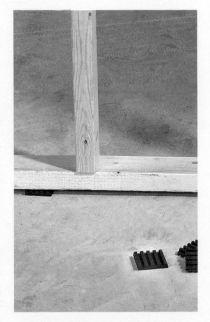

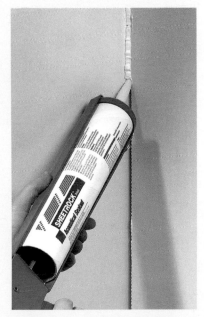

Staple MLV (mass loaded vinyl) underlayment directly to framing members, between layers of wallboard and soundproofing board, or directly to existing wall and ceiling surfaces. Overlap seams by at least 6".

Install 2" vibration pads every 2 feet between wall sole plates and subfloor (nonloadbearing walls only). Fasten baseboard into framing only, not into vibration pads.

Seal all gaps between panels and at wall and ceiling joints with acoustical caulk.

Routing Cables & Wires

Routing cable and wire of any kind requires drilling holes through framing members throughout the home. Drill holes no closer than 2 inches from the top or bottom edge of joists. Use nail plates to protect holes in studs within 2 inches of the edge. Always check your local building codes for requirements in your area.

Low-voltage cable can run a maximum of 295 ft. from the distribution center without any significant signal loss. The cable cannot run within 6 inches of electrical wires and can cross only from a 90-degree angle.

To route cables and wires, begin at the outlet bracket or box locations, and feed to the distribution center. The maximum allowable pulling tension for UTP cable is 25 pounds. Use electrical tape to hold the tips of all cables and wires together as they are fed, and avoid knots and kinks. Leave at least 12 inches of slack at bracket or box locations for making connections.

If your service connections are outside the home, drill 1-inch holes through to the outside near the service entrance location. Insert a 1-inch PVC conduit, and feed cables and wires through it. Leave 36 inches of slack, and attach notice tags to the ends for utility workers.

At the distribution center, mark each cable and wire according to its routing location. Feed each through the top of the enclosure, and cut the lead ends so they hang even with the bottom of the distribution center. When routing is complete, tuck all cables and wires neatly inside the distribution center and finish wall construction.

Tools & Materials ▸

Drill	Cables
Crimp tool	RJ45 plugs
Tape	F-connectors

Drill 1" holes through the top plate above the distribution center. Drill holes in floor joists for running cable along the underside of house levels and from the service entrance to the distribution center. When possible, locate the distribution center in the theater room.

Label each run of cable and wire at the distribution center with the room and location within the room. All cables should hang even with the bottom of the distribution center.

How to Attach RJ45 Plugs to a UTP Cable

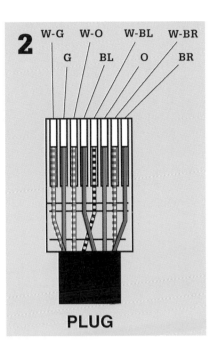

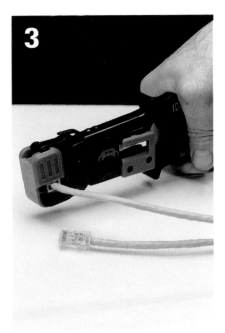

Strip 1 to 2" of outer insulation from the UTP cable. Separate the twisted pairs of individual wires.

Straighten and arrange each of the wires in order, according to the wiring assignment chart. Trim the ends evenly to ½" from the outer insulation. Insert the wires into the grooves of an RJ45 plug.

Make sure each wire is under the proper IDC (the conductor ends of the RJ45 plug) and that the outer insulation is ½" inside the plug. Crimp the plug with a RJ45 crimp tool.

How to Attach F-connectors to Coaxial Cable

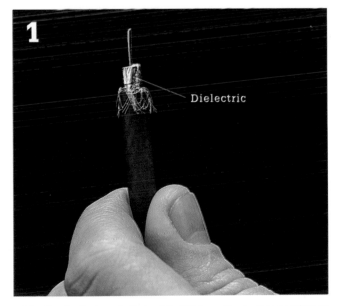

Strip the jacket and dielectric ⅜" from the center conductor. Strip the jacket ¼" from the foil and braid.

Slide the metal F-connector on until the dielectric is flush with the center barrel. The center conductor should extend ¹⁄₁₆" past the end of the F-connector. Crimp the outer barrel of the connector to the cable jacket, using an F-connector crimp tool.

Installing Recessed Wall Speakers

High-quality audio speakers have shrunk in size in recent years, to the point where it's possible to have the convenience of recessed speakers without sacrificing sound fidelity.

Even though speakers are smaller today, an ideal wall for recess mounting should be 6 inches thick or more. A soffit above the entertainment equipment is a good choice for recessing speakers, but you should install them as low on the wall as you can.

Tools & Materials ▸

Screwdriver
Speaker mounting brackets
Screws
Volume control box
Speakers

Eliminate clutter and unsightliness by installing speakers in recesses that you cut into the home theater wall or wall façade. Most electronics stores sell speakers that have metal mounting brackets but not cabinets.

How to Install a Recessed Speaker System

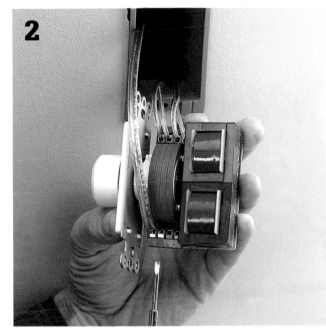

Attach the speaker mounting brackets to the metal crossrail and then attach the rails to the wall studs at the ends of the opening you cut in the wallcovering. Patch around the opening with new wallcovering material.

Run speaker wires to the volume control (if you're installing one), with positive to positive (+ or red) and negative to negative (– or black). Position the module in the gang box, and screw into place. Attach the coverplate.

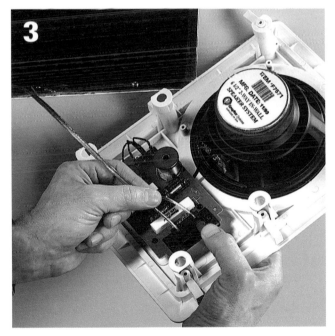

Connect the wires at each speaker. Keep positive to positive (+ or red) and negative to negative (– or black). Attach the speaker to the bracket. Some recessed speakers have plastic mounting arms that swing into place and clamp to the bracket when the front screws are tightened. Follow the manufacturer's directions.

Alternate Method: If you're not installing a recessed speaker system, install speaker binding posts. The network speaker wire is connected to the back of the binding posts. Run positive to positive (+ or red) and negative to negative (– or black).

Installing Acoustic Ceiling Tile

Ceiling tiles made of pressed mineral and fiberboard are available in a variety of styles. Installing these tiles is a fairly simple project that will help soundproof your entertainment room.Ceiling tiles typically can be attached directly to a drywall or plaster ceiling with adhesive. If your ceiling is damaged or uneven or if you have an unfinished joist ceiling, install 1 × 2 furring strips as a base for the tiles, as shown in this project. Some systems include metal tracks for clip-on installation.

Unless your ceiling measures in even feet, you won't be able to install the 12-inch tiles without some cutting. To prevent an unattractive installation with small, irregular tiles along two sides, include a course of border tiles along the perimeter of the installation. Plan so that tiles at opposite ends of the room are cut to the same width and are at least one-half the width of a full tile.

Most ceiling tile comes prefinished, but it can be painted to match any decor. For best results, apply two coats of paint using a roller with a ¼" nap, and wait 24 hours between coats.

Tools & Materials ▸

4-ft. level	Stapler
Stepladder	1 × 2 furring strips
Chalk line	8d nails or 2" screws
Utility knife	String
Straightedge	Ceiling tiles
Hammer or drill	Staples
Handsaw	Trim molding

Acoustic tile improves the sound quality inside a home theater and reduces the transmission of sound to the rooms surrounding it.

Planning a Layout ▸

Measure the ceiling and devise a layout. If the length (or width) doesn't measure in even feet, use this formula to determine the width of the border tiles: add 12 to the number of inches remaining and divide by 2. The result is the width of the border tile. (For example, if the room length is 15 ft., 4", add 12 to the 4, then divide 16 by 2, which results in an 8" border tile.)

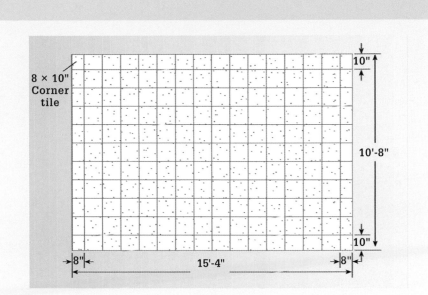

8 × 10" Corner tile

10"

10'-8"

10"

8"

15'-4"

8"

How to Install an Acoustic Tile Ceiling

Tip ▸

Acoustic tiles are generally made from cellulose fibers with a textured facing of vinyl. You can buy suspended ceiling tiles with sound deadening properties, but true acoustic tiles are mounted to strips or channels that are attached directly to the ceiling. Above are a few design styles.

1

Install the first furring strip flush with the wall and perpendicular to the joists, fastening with two 8d nails or 2" screws at each joist. Measure out from the wall a distance equal to the border tile width minus ¾", and snap a chalk line. Install the second furring strip with its wall-side edge on the chalk line.

(continued)

2

Install the remaining strips 12" on-center from the second strip. Measure from the second strip and mark the joist nearest the wall every 12". Repeat along the joist on the opposite side of the room, then snap chalk lines between the marks. Install the furring strips along the lines. Install the last furring strip flush against the opposite side wall. Stagger the butted end joints of strips between rows so they aren't all on the same joist.

Check the strips with a 4-ft. level. Insert wood shims between the strips and joists as necessary to bring the strips into a level plane.

Set up taut, perpendicular string lines along two adjacent walls to help guide the tile installation. Inset the strings from the wall by a distance that equals that wall's border tile width plus ½". Use a framing square to make sure the strings are square.

5

Cut the corner border tile to size with a utility knife and straightedge. Cutting the border tiles ¼" short will ease fitting them. The resulting gap between the tile and wall will be covered by trim. Cut only on the edges without the stapling flange.

6

Position the corner tile with the flange edges aligned with the two string lines and fasten it to the furring strips with four ½" staples. Cut and install two border tiles along each wall, making sure the tiles fit snugly together.

7

Fill in between the border tiles with full size tiles. Continue working diagonally in this manner toward the opposite corner. For the border tiles along the far wall, trim off the flange edges and staple through the faces of the tiles, close to the wall.

8

Install the final row of tiles, saving the far corner tile and its neighbor for last. Cut the last tile to size, then remove the tongue and nailing flange along the side edges. Finish the job by installing trim along the edges.

Building Media Display Storage

Simple wood boxes clad with quartz tile form columns for this impressive display and storage space.

A wall niche—a recessed area between studs—provides ideal media display space and creates a focal point in a room. Recessed niches require special framing, and if you're working with existing construction you have to cut into the wall to reach it. Cutting into a wall isn't difficult but can be a little intimidating if you haven't done it before. The answer's simple—build out rather than in.

The "columns" that form the sides of our niche are plain wood boxes that are built in a workshop and then installed. Quartz tile is attached to the columns after installation, and contrasting wall tiles are added to the wallspace between the columns. Finally, glass shelves are installed between the tiled columns to complete the project. The finished look is textural, natural, and sophisticated.

When designing your project, consider the size of the tile and grout lines to create a plan that requires the fewest possible cut tiles. If it's not possible to complete an area (such as a column or the background) with full tile, plan to cut equal-size tiles for each side so the full tiles are centered. If it is not possible for you to attach both boxes to wall studs, use sturdy hollow wall anchors or toggle bolts to secure one of the boxes.

Tools & Materials ▸

Tape measure	(4) 1 × 8
Stud finder	1¼" Phillips
Circular saw	or square-head
Drill	screws
Long driver bit	Construction
or bit extender	adhesive
Bar clamps	Wide painter's tape
Pry bar	Sheet plastic tile
Hammer	Thinset mortar
Level	Tile spacers
Awl	Grout
¼" carbide-tip bit	Latex additive
¼" notched trowel	Straight 2 × 2 scraps
Grout float	for battens
Grout sponge	Shelf pins
Buff rag	(4 per shelf)
Foam brush	Teflon tape
Needlenose pliers	Glass shelves
Rubber mallet	Grout sealer
(4) 1 × 6	

How to Build a Tiled Wall Niche

Measure the area and draw a plan on graph paper. Use a stud finder to locate the studs in the area and mark them.

If there are baseboards in the construction area, remove them, using a pry bar and hammer. Tape down sheet plastic in the construction area, as close to the wall as possible.

(continued)

3

Cut four 1 × 6s and four 1 × 8s to length (108" for our project). On two of the 1 × 8s, drill ¾" holes centered every 10" down the length of each board. On the remaining two 1 × 8s, drill pilot holes centered every 10".

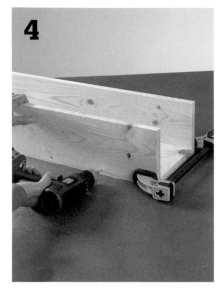

4

Place one 1 × 8 (one with pilot holes) on the work surface and position a 1 × 6 on each edge. Clamp the boards together and drive a 1¼" screw every 6" to join the sides to the bottom.

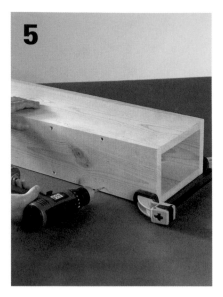

5

Complete the box by adding a 1 × 8 to the opposite side of the assembly and fasten it as described in step 4. Build a second, identical box.

6

Shoot a vertical line on the wall with the laser level. Spread a bead of construction adhesive on the back (1 × 8 with pilot holes) of the first box. With a helper, align the outside edge of the box. Using a long magnetic driver bit or bit extender, drive a 1½" or 1⅝" screw through each pilot hole (and into stud). Install the second box on the other side of the niche. *Note: When you cannot hit a stud, use toggle bolts.*

7

Mark the reference lines. If necessary, tack a 1 × 2 batten in position to support the second row of tile above the floor. If tiles have to be cut for this row, mark and cut all of them.

8

Mix a small batch of thinset mortar. Spread the mortar on a small section of wall, then set the tiles into it. If the tile is not self-spacing, insert spacers as you work. When all other tile is set and the thinset mortar has thoroughly cured, remove the battens and set the bottom row.

9

Repeat Step 8 to set tile on first one box and then the other. Let the mortar cure, according to manufacturer's instructions.

10

If there are spacers between tiles, use needlenose pliers to remove them. Grout the tile in the center of the niche If necessary, and grout the tile on the columns. (The type of tile shown here does not get grouted.) Let the grout set and then wipe away excess with a damp sponge.

11

On the inside edges of each column, measure and mark the location for the shelf pins. Use a laser level to check and adjust the marks. Using an awl and hammer, create a dimple at each mark, then use a carbide-tipped ¼" bit to drill the holes.

12

Wrap the peg of each shelf pin with tape. (The tape will seal the hole and keep moisture from getting behind the tile.) Tap a pin into each hole, using a rubber mallet if necessary. Position the glass shelves.

DIY Projection Theater

If you want The Big Screen to be a literal quality of your home theater, you'll want to consider a front-projection TV. Historically, projection televisions have suffered a bit from their low-resolution reputation, but new digital technology has lead to a revolution in this television category. Today, front-projection TVs can project a sharp, crisp image that's as big as 10 feet wide. And best of all, along with the advances in quality have come a reduction in size, simplification of maintenance and use, and a significant reduction in cost.

Front-projection TVs can be set on a coffee table, tucked away in a cabinet, or even mounted to the ceiling. Similarly, the screens they project onto can be the roll-down type we know from elementary school, or they can be permanently affixed to the wall, often hidden behind curtains.

In this section you'll find some information on buying and operating a front-projection television. You'll also see some tips on how to set up an optimal viewing environment, and we'll even show you two ways you can save hundreds of dollars by making your own pro-quality screen from scratch.

Front-projection systems project images as big as 10 ft. wide, with excellent quality.

Terms You Should Know ▸

Aspect ratio: The aspect ratio refers to the proportions of the projected image. Standard televisions project a 4:3 aspect ratio image (4 units wide to 3 units high). Many newer models (high-definition TV in particular) use the narrower 16:9 ratio (16 units wide to 9 units high), which is based on a typical motion picture screen shape. Most home projection theaters have a native 16:9 ratio because they tend to feature movies that were originally shot in this mode. But if you intend to use your theater for viewing TV or recordings of shows shot for TV, you should look into the 4:3 aspect ratio.

Resolution: The resolution of a projector refers to the maximum number of image pixels it can produce: the more pixels, the crisper the image. Among digital projectors, you have three typical resolution options available. The numbers noted refer to the number of available pixels in a horizontal line by the number in a vertical line.

854 by 480 ("480p"): These are relatively low-resolution projectors, but the 480 pixels in the vertical line matches the output of regular TV or DVD, so if you don't plan to get into the high-definition game, this entry-level projector may work for you. Prices start around $500.

1280 by 720 ("720p"): The most common resolution for 16:9 home projectors, they can handle high-definition digital signals and many are quite affordable, starting around $1,000.

1920 by 1080 ("1080p"): The sharpest picture quality available, these ultra-high definition projectors are designed to handle HD DVD and Blu-ray discs without any image degradation. Plan on spending at least $4,000 to $5,000.

Brightness, contrast, and throw are other variables you should acquaint yourself with if you're looking into a higher end projector.

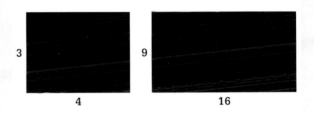

Front-Projection TVs

When you think of projection televisions, you probably have in mind three large colored lenses in a box the size of a small refrigerator. Known as CRT projectors, these models generally require professional installation and are quite expensive. But the digital revolution has impacted the world of front-projection TVs. Today, the projector market is being taken over by digital projectors in a variety of formats. The most common is

LCD (liquid crystal display), a technology that is also being used extensively in rear-projection televisions. A slightly more expensive digital format is DLP (digital light processing), a proprietary technology owned by Texas Instruments. With the new technology, projectors have been trimmed down to as small as five pounds, making them portable and more flexible for home use.

Today's smaller, more affordable front-projection systems offer excellent crisp images and are easily installed.

Setting Up a Projection Theater

While a home theater with a rear-projection TV can easily perform multiple functions, when you invest in a front-projection theater you should plan on giving it a dedicated space. This is mainly because a projection theater should be dark when in use. If your home theater goals are to watch television or socialize, you may want to go with a traditional large-screen TV. The room you choose will also have a bearing on the maximum size screen you can use. The ideal room, then, is rectangular, at least 12 feet long in one dimension, and windowless or easily darkened.

It's a good idea to have a specific spot in mind for your projector before you purchase it. Some models project in a wider angle that works well in short distances, making them a good choice for use when set on a coffee table in a small room. Other models have a longer "throw distance" that makes them more suitable for ceiling mounting at the back of the room.

Ultimately, the size of the room and the type of projector determine just how large a screen you'll need. It isn't hard to calculate the appropriate screen size using the specs for your projector and your known room size. But a sure way to know you're getting the correct screen for your needs is to buy the projector, set it up, and measure the image size. Then you can order a projection screen, or you may choose to make your own. You can also use a white or light gray wall, but the image quality will suffer quite a bit compared to a screen.

Tip: Projectors are image-output devices, and that's it. When you set up your projection theater, you'll need to accommodate input devices like a DVD player and a TV receiver to provide signals to the projector (which can be a bit of a tangle if you choose to ceiling-mount the projector). You'll also need to provide a sound output device, presumably your home theater sound system, to connect to your signal source.

Tools & Materials ▸

Joint compound
10" taping knife
Sanding screen for joint compound
Masking tape
Paint roller with short-nap (⅜") sleeve

1 gallon screen paint (Behr SilverScreen paint, 770E-2)
(1) 2" × 35 ft. roll FLOK (see Resources)

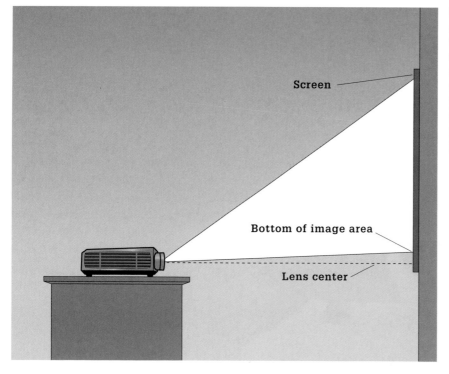

Projectors beam out an offset image so the image won't be obstructed by the table the projector is sitting on or the ceiling it is mounted to. The degree of offset can usually be manipulated within a limited range to conform to your preferences for screen height and mounting height. However, using the maximum offset can cause some image distortion.

Screen

Bottom of image area

Lens center

How to Turn a Wall into a Screen

1

2

Calculate your screen size using your projector specifications and room size and desired aspect ratio. Or, set up your projector in the position you want it, turn it on, and measure the image size. In the project shown here, a 16:9 aspect ratio screen that's 4½ ft. high and 8 ft. wide is being laid out with masking tape (that's a 9.179 ft. diagonal picture!).

Fix any holes, bulges, or cracks in the screen area and then coat the area inside the masking tape with joint compound, using a wide joint taping knife. Get the surface as smooth as you possibly can. Once it dries, sand it lightly. If it is not smooth, reapply and re-sand until it is.

3

4

Using a short-nap paint roller sleeve, paint the masked area with oil-based primer, let it dry, and then cover with two light coats of screen paint. There are several paints with reflective qualities on the market that are formulated to be used as a movie screen surface (see Resources). Try to get the surface perfectly smooth.

Carefully remove the tape. Because the image will look dramatically better if the screen has a dark frame, frame it. You can use wood molding painted with flat black paint if you wish. Here, a specialty tape called Flok is being applied. Apply it straight and miter the corners. Your screen is finished. If you like, hang a curtain over it.

How to Make a Hanging Picture Screen

Masking tape
1 × 4 pine

Black felt
1 can spray adhesive

53"-wide roll of
  white photo paper

(4) ¾" × 8' screen retainer strips
Picture hanger hook

If you don't wish to create a screen directly on your walls, as on the previous page, you can build a hanging projection screen. Start by calculating the size of the screen using your projector specifications and room size or by projecting an image on the wall and measuring it.

Cut boards for a wood screen frame. The frame should have mitered corners, and the inside dimensions once the frame is built should equal the picture size. The frame being built here will have inside dimensions of 4 ft. high and 7 ft. wide.

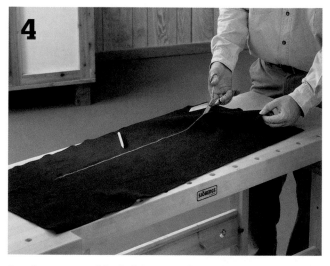

Assemble the frame with finish nails or pneumatic nails and glue. Measure the distance between opposite corners to determine squareness. Adjust as necessary to make the distances equal.

Purchase some black felt to apply to the frame. The felt will not reflect light and greatly improves the perceived picture quality. Cut it into strips that are slightly longer than each frame board and wide enough to wrap around the back, concealing the front faces and the edges.

Apply a light coat of spray adhesive to the front face of the frame, one side at a time. Carefully set the felt into the adhesive, stretching it tight. Using a straightedge guide, cut the ends of the felt with a craft knife, following the miter joint lines in the frame. Flip the frame over, draw the loose ends flat, and staple them to the back faces of the frame.

Purchase some white photographers paper at a professional photography supplies store. Sold in 53"-wide rolls, this paper has treated surfaces that reflect light and show color very naturally. Cut the paper so it's slightly smaller than the outside dimensions of the frame, then attach it to the frame by nailing screen retainer strips around the perimeter of the frame. Start at the top, and then draw the paper taut as you attach the bottom strip. Do the sides last.

Attach a sturdy picture hanger to the back of the frame. The hanger should be centered exactly. Make sure to use a hanger that will be concealed by the frame.

Hang the screen on the wall. If the screen cannot be located so the hanger will be attached to a wall stud, use a wall anchor to secure the hanging screw.

Cigar Lounge Projects

It's Saturday night—time to unwind, time to enjoy the fruits of your labor. Time, in fact, to indulge in a glass of brandy and a good cigar. You lift the lid on your humidor and inhale the fragrance. There, in all its hand-rolled elegance, is your cigar collection. You select a favorite, sink into your comfortable leather chair, and set about enjoying the ritual of lighting a truly fine cigar.

No more cold nights on the deck, no more lawn chairs in the garage. With a smoking lounge in the house, you've got more than a comfortable place to smoke—you've got a retreat from the rest of the world.

As antismoking legislation sweeps the world, smokers are finding their cigarettes and cigars welcome in fewer and fewer places. The logical move is to take refuge in their own homes, but many smokers share space with nonsmokers or children, and they don't want to expose their loved ones to the smoke or the smell. This chapter provides information and projects that will help you create a smoking lounge that protects family members and the house. The projects will help you seal the lounge off from the rest of the house, provide proper ventilation within it, and create an atmosphere conducive to enjoying the finer things in life.

In This Chapter:
- Gallery of Cigar Lounges
- All About Cigar Lounges
- Sealing a Room
- Installing an Exhaust Fan
- Building a Humidor
- Building a Poker Table

Gallery of Cigar Lounges

A gentleman's gentleman is the only thing missing from this elegant room. What a beautiful place to relax with a cigar at the end of a long day.

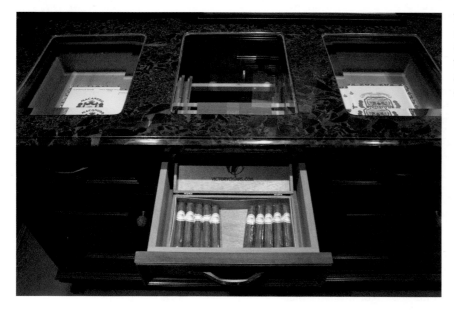

This is more than a place to store a cigar collection, it's a celebration of the art of collecting. The deep drawers are topped with glass insets so the cigars can be admired, while the doors below conceal other accoutrements.

A fireplace is a welcome addition to a smoking lounge. So are deep-cushioned leather chairs and ottomans.

Don't rule out the outdoors quite yet! This outdoor room offers special advantages for smokers. The sheltered area has all the comforts of an indoor lounge, plus excellent ventilation.

Operable windows contribute fresh air and ventilation, critical to a comfortable smoking lounge. Impermeable window coverings are best, as they don't absorb smoke and odors. Wooden shutters, such as the ones shown here, are ideal.

Even a small ceiling vent fan makes a big difference in keeping the air moving in your smoking lounge. Ideally, you should try and move at least 60 cubic feet per minute of air per smoker.

The fresh air and ambient light available in sunrooms and other rooms with entrance doors make them excellent choices for a smoking lounge.

All About Cigar Lounges

Generally speaking, cigar lounges are luxuriously appointed rooms with comfortable seating, low lighting, and perhaps a game table, card table, or pool table. Smoke containment, washability, and ventilation are their key physical features. There are no real limitations as to where in the house the cigar lounge should be located, but where possible put it next to your formal dining area. This will allow you to retire to the lounge for a nice cigar and perhaps a snifter of brandy after a fine repaste.

Good ventilation, nonabsorbent, easily cleaned surfaces, and outrageous comfort are hallmarks of a successful smoking lounge.

Smoke Containment

A primary reason for dedicating an entire room to smoking is so you can contain the smoke within the room, allowing it to be vented outdoors before it migrates throughout the house. This is largely a matter of sealing gaps around interior openings, like doors, receptacles, and baseboards. These projects, primarily accomplished with familiar weatherstripping and insulating products, are quick, easy, and inexpensive. See "Sealing a Room," pages 86 to 87.

Door weatherstripping products are used to create a smoke-proof seal on the interior door leading into the cigar lounge.

Ventilation

Opening a window is, naturally, an effective way to exhaust smoke, especially the venting process with a window fan. But for a number of reasons, natural ventilation should be viewed only as supplemental to mechanical ventilation in your smoking lounge.

The most obvious solution to a smoking lounge's ventilation issues is to install an exhaust fan similar to a bathroom vent fan, but more powerful. Typical bathroom vent fans move around 60 cubic feet per minute of air. More powerful fans, such as wall-mounted utility fans, are as quiet and can move double the amount of air or even more. In the vent fan project shown in this chapter (see pages 88 to 91), we replace a ceiling light with a combination vent fan/ceiling light that provides ventilation without sacrificing appearance. Because smoke tends to rise, a ceiling-mounted fan is a good fit for a cigar lounge.

Consider adding an electronic timer to your fan so you can let the fan continue exhausting the air for a bit after you've moved on to other activities.

A healthful addition to any room is a fan or air purifier (the one shown here is cleverly concealed under a ceiling light and integrated into an HVAC system that serves the entire house). See Resources (page 238). Other variations are available.

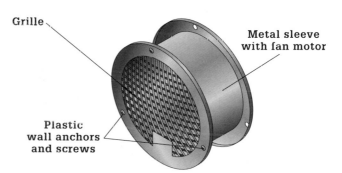

Integrating a wall fan to circulate and filter air between rooms is a simple DIY project that will drastically improve the atmosphere in an interior smoking lounge. Such fans can be installed within walls and doors.

Walls

The walls in your cigar lounge should be washable, but that doesn't mean you're limited to only hard surfaces like ceramic tile or plastic tileboard. In fact, these materials are not really conducive to establishing an elegant, restful retreat. Paint is one obvious and very versatile wall treatment, but traditionally only harder, enamel surfaces (and usually only oil-base) are truly scrubbable. And anyone who has ever tried washing a wall that's coated with flat latex wall paint knows what a mess that can make.

The solution is washable wall paint. Several manufacturers have developed satin or even flat wall paints that have a hard enough surface to stand up to the dreaded wet sponge. Available as tint bases, these easy-cleaning paints can be mixed to any color you choose.

Tip ▸

Solid-vinyl wallpapers are another good smoking room wallcovering. As opposed to vinyl-coated papers, these are solid plastic, which makes them easy to wipe down with warm water. Look for the prepasted papers.

Yet another option is to panel the wall with paneling that has a washable wear layer over the photo laminate. You can also use real wood paneling and apply a topcoat of polyurethane or varnish.

Washing Walls & Ceilings ▸

A mild detergent and water solution works just fine for regular cleaning. Wipe walls with a rag or sponge, working from top to bottom and rinsing the rag or sponge frequently. You can also make your own natural cleaner that is very effective for cutting smoke residue. The ingredients are:

- 1 cup household ammonia
- ½ cup white vinegar
- ¼ cup baking soda
- 1 gallon warm water

Mix the ammonia, white vinegar, and baking soda in a bucket and then add the warm water. With this cleaner, you should work from the bottom up toward the top of the wall, and wring the sponge or rag out each time you rinse so you don't get runoff. You shouldn't have to rinse the wall or ceiling with clean water when you're done washing it.

Wash stains with water and mild detergent, using a sponge.

Ceilings

Most of the information in the previous discussion of walls also applies to suitable ceiling coverings for cigar lounges. However, there are a number of common ceiling treatments you should avoid in a smoking area. Because you'll need to clean the ceiling regularly, do not apply a textured surface (such as the ubiquitous popcorn ceilings of the 60s and 70s). Most suspended ceilings and acoustical tile ceilings are not well suited, even if they are painted with washable paint. Ceiling tile that is coated with vinyl is okay to use, just use a light touch on the moisture when washing—water can get into the joints between tiles easily.

Another ceiling material you'll want to avoid is metal ceiling panels. Because they have hard surfaces they would seem to be a good choice for smoking rooms, but most actual metal ceiling panels are exceptionally difficult to keep clean unless they have been painted.

Most ceiling tiles, including suspended ceilings and acoustical tiles, are not easy to clean and therefore don't work well in a cigar lounge. Once exception is vinyl-coated ceiling tiles, like the ones above.

Floors

The same basic rules apply for floors as for walls and ceilings: you want a covering that is easy to clean and won't trap odors. A hardwood or laminate floor is a good alternative, and you can soften it a bit with washable area rugs. Low-pile wall-to-wall carpeting is not ideal, but some people prefer it. It should be steam cleaned at least once a year, however, depending on use.

Avoid carpeting or rugs with a thick pile. Also stay away from materials that melt easily and are hard to repair, such as sheet vinyl (not a particularly appealing material for a cigar lounge anyway). Easy to clean and hard to singe, ceramic tile and stone have many advantages for a smoking area. Their only downside is that you may find them a bit cold and uninviting.

Painted wood makes a great material for cigar lounge window coverings. Venetian blinds and plantation shutters (above) are two good wood options.

Window Treatments

Avoid using heavy draperies to cover windows in a cigar room, even though they may have just the look you want. Most of the more velvet-like coverings require professional cleaning. Lightweight curtains, especially machine-washable ones, are acceptable but not ideal. Vinyl rolldown window shades and plastic or metal mini-blinds don't absorb odors nor do they stain easily. But they're not especially attractive room additions.

For the ultimate cigar lounge window treatment, install wooden Venetian blinds or plantation shutters. Preferably, paint them with enamel paint to make them easier to clean.

Furnishings

If your budget and taste allow it, choose sofas and chairs upholstered in leather—their surfaces don't absorb smoke the way fabrics do. Small side tables with granite or marble tops are excellent choices for positioning next to a nice club chair. Choose lamp shades made of glass or another hard material.

For furnishings too, nonabsorbent and washable surfaces are important qualities to consider when appointing your lounge.

Smoking Accessories

Because a cigar lounge is a specialty room, you'll want to include some specialty items related to its functions. In addition to decorative elements like cigar store statuary or vintage tobacco posters, you'll want to include some practical items. Matchboxes, novelty lighters, a cigar clip, a pipe reamer … there are many to choose from. Most importantly, of course, you'll want several ashtrays. These can be fun and decorative or hardworking and practical, such as "smokeless" ashtrays that have built-in ionizing air filters.

Tobacco-themed art and antique furniture enhances the mood of the environment and, in some cases, these items are highly collectible.

Cigar clippers do a neat job of snipping off the tip of the cigar before smoking.

A "smokeless" ashtray provides yet another line of defense against secondhand smoke.

Humidity-controlled cigar storage boxes not only maintain quality but they can stand in as stylish accessories throughout the room.

Sealing a Room

Containing smoking odors allows smokers to peacefully coexist with nonsmokers, which is one of the fundamental reasons for building a smoking lounge. Seal around all sides of doors that lead into the living areas of the house, and look for other areas in common walls where smoke can migrate out.

Tools & Materials ▸

Carpenter's level
Tape measure
Hacksaw and drill
Self-adhesive, closed-cell foam tape
   and door sweep

Tip ▸

Seal walls with weatherstripping and insulating products, such as foam gaskets that fit between wall receptacles and switches and their coverplates.

Sealing the edges of the doors protects the rest of the house from the smoke and odor of a smoking lounge.

How to Seal an Interior Door

Cut strips of closed-cell foam tape to fit on the door side of the doorstop molding. Pull the backing off the foam tape and press it onto the doorframe.

Purchase a rubber door sweep for the door bottom. Working from inside the room, measure the width of the door. Mark a cutting line on the hinge side of the door sweep and hold it against the door to check the measurement. Cut the sweep to size, using a hacksaw or another tool if recommended by the manufacturer

With the door closed, place the door sweep against the door with the bottom of the sweep just touching the door threshold or floor. The bottom of the sweep should barely be making contact with the floor. Trace the top of the sweep onto the door with a pencil.

Hold the sweep in position while you mark the screw positions. Drill pilot holes (consult manufacturer's instructions for screw size). Drive a screw at each end to hold the sweep in place, and then open and close the door to check the sweep's position. It should barely graze the floor, but still open and close with little effort. Install the remaining screws.

Installing an Exhaust Fan

Good ventilation is essential to a comfortable lounge. Adding an exhaust fan to the room is a project that will pay huge returns on your investment of time and energy. Select a fan sized to provide adequate ventilation for the square footage of your smoking lounge. According to The Home Ventilating Institute, the air in rooms other than kitchens and bathrooms should be replaced at least six times per hour. Another calculation method uses a ratio of 70 cubic feet minimum per smoker. If you plan to host your local cigar afficionado's club on a regular basis, don't use 12 as your multiplier unless you're ready to invest in some restaurant-grade air moving equipment. The volume of smoke produced is a more accurate guide than the volume of air. These are, of course, minimums. You might want to discuss your smoking lounge with an HVAC expert before selecting an exhaust fan.

The exhaust fan installed in this project is a ceiling-mounted unit with a light socket and a decorative diffuser (see Resources, page 236). It is stylish and a perfect fixture for a one-for-one replacement with an existing overhead light.

Because this project requires working with electricity, be cautious. Shut off power to the circuit and test outlets before you begin.

Tools & Materials ▸

Phillips and straight screwdrivers
Jigsaw or drywall saw
Reciprocating saw
Drill
Electrical tester
Exhaust fan unit
Drywall screws

Self-sealing roofing nails
Wire connectors
Flexible dryer vent duct
Dryer vent clamps
Vent cover
Drywall

An exhaust fan provides ventilation that is critical to a smoking lounge.

How to Replace an Overhead Light with a Light/Fan

1

Shut off power to the ceiling light at the electrical service panel. Remove the globe and bulb from the overhead ceiling light, and then disconnect the mounting screws that hold the light fixture to the ceiling box.

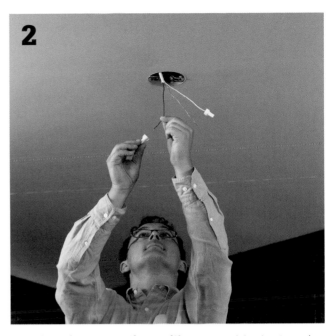

2

Test the wire connections with a current tester to make sure they are not live, and then disconnect the wires and remove the light fixture. Cap the wire ends.

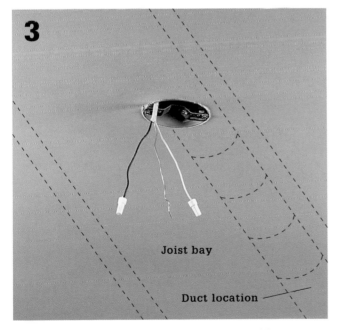

3

Joist bay

Duct location

Plan your exhaust pipe route. In most cases, this means determining the shortest distance between the fan and the outdoors. If the room is located at the top living level, venting through the roof is usually smartest. On lower levels and in basements, you'll need to go through an exterior wall. If you need to route through a wall in a room with a finished ceiling, choose a route that runs through a single ceiling joist bay.

4

Remove ceiling covering in the fan unit installation area and between the joists at the end of the run, next to the wall. You'll need at least 18" of access. If you are running rigid vent pipe or the joist bay is insulated, you'll need to remove ceiling material between the joists for the entire run. Make cuts on the centerlines of the joists.

(continued)

5

Insert flexible vent tubing into one of the ceiling openings and expand it so the free end reaches to the ceiling opening at the wall. A fish-tape for running cable through walls can be a useful aid for extending the tubing.

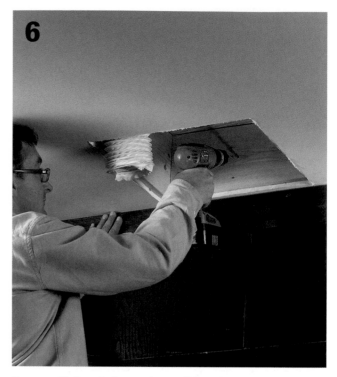

6

Draw a 4"-dia. circle on the wall framing at the end of the joist bay, marking the exit point for the duct. Choose a long, ¼"-dia. drill bit and drill a hole at the center of the circle. Drill all the way through the wall so the bit exits on the exterior side. This will mark your hole location outside.

7

On the exterior, draw a 4"-dia. circle centered on the exit point of the drill bit. Cut out the opening for the vent cover with a reciprocating saw (or a 4" hole saw if you can find one).

8

Insert the vent cover assembly into the opening, following the manufacturer's directions for fastening and sealing it to the house.

9

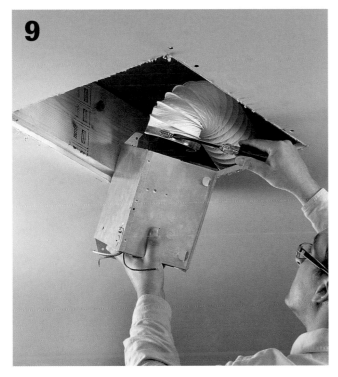

Attach the end of the vent tubing to the outlet on the vent cover unit and secure it with a large pipe clamp.

10

Nail the housing for the light/fan unit to the ceiling joist so the bottom edges of the housing are flush with the ceiling surface.

11

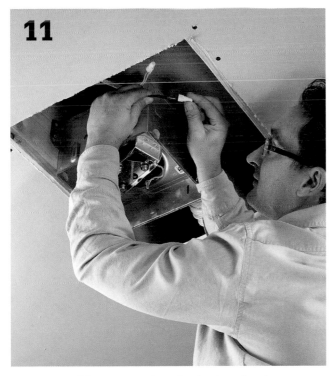

Make the wiring connections in the housing box according to the manufacturer's instructions. In just about every case you should be able to use the existing wires from the original light switch. Once you have connected the wires, restore the power and test the fan.

12

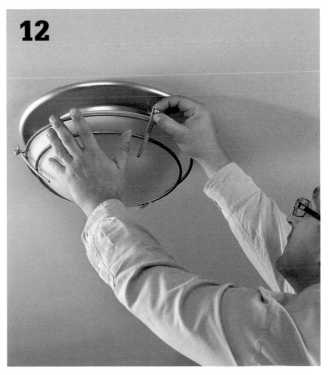

Patch and paint the wall and ceiling in the project area as shown on page 125. Mount the light (the model we installed plugs into a receptacle in the fan box), grille, globe, and any other fixture parts.

Building a Humidor

Even the world's best cigars become stale, dry, and virtually unsmokeable if they are not stored properly. For this reason, most serious cigar enthusiasts keep their stash of stogies in a humidor. Humidors are sealed containers with controllable humidity levels. They range from small travel sizes that hold just a handful of cigars to larger case-style humidors that can hold several hundred cigars.

Larger, fancier humidors rely on electrically powered, automatic humidifiers to maintain ideal relative humidity levels. Smaller models use cruder methods, such as absorbent beads, to raise humidity levels.

This project shows you how to turn a regular picnic cooler into a cigar humidor. A slatted wood floor and stackable wood trays allow you to store your cigars in their original wood cigar boxes (remove the cover) or individually in the trays. To make the wood floor and trays, use Spanish cedar—an aromatic wood that's valued by cigar aficionados all over the world because it readily absorbs excess humidity and also imparts a pleasant flavor to the tobacco. Some online exotic wood suppliers sell Spanish cedar. Most full-service lumberyards do as well. The wood deck and the drawers are designed so almost all parts can be made with Spanish cedar that's been milled to ⅜ inches thick and ripped to 2½ inches wide. You'll also need a few feet of ¾ × ¾ stock, preferably Spanish cedar as well.

Using a handful of materials, a picnic cooler can be transformed into an attractive, efficient humidor.

The relative humidity inside a humidor should be between 68 percent and 70 percent. A device called a hygrometer monitors humidity levels. To control humidity inside the humidor, use humidity beads. Humidity beads (the ones shown here are made of silica gel) are sprayed with distilled water and set into the humidor in a shallow dish, where they gradually release the water as humidity. When they dry out they change color and you spray them again.

This project calls for a small, battery-operated fan. An Oust air freshener fan is ideal as long as you do not add the fragrance, which would ruin your cigars. To make the fan more effective, remove the small screws holding the cover on the fan and remove it. For our humidor, we built a simple stand for it to give it a bit more presence.

Tools & Materials ▶

Miter saw
Hammer
Jigsaw
54-quart
    picnic cooler
⅜ × 2½"
    Spanish cedar
4-ft. ¾ × ¾"
    Spanish cedar
1" brass brads

Cigar
    humidity beads
Hygrometer
1 × 4 cherry,
    ¾" hardwood
    plywood scrap
Battery-operated
    air freshener fan

How to Build a Picnic Cooler Humidor

Measure the width, length, and height of the cooler's interior. Wash the walls of the cooler with soapy water. Rinse it thoroughly and leave it open to dry. Put a small bowl filled with baking soda inside to absorb odors as the cooler dries.

Prepare the Spanish cedar stock for the humidor floor and stacking trays. Plane the stock to ⅜" thick and rip it into 2½"-wide strips. If you do not have woodworking equipment, the lumberyard where you purchase the wood can mill it for you for a charge.

Make the floor for the cooler. The slats should run parallel to the cooler front, stopping about ½" from each end. The ¾ × ¾" supports should be cut to be about 1" shorter than the front-to-back distance on the interior of the cooler. Cut the parts to length.

(continued)

Assemble the floor as if it were a mini deck. Lay the supports parallel to one another on a flat work surface, with one about 1" from each end and another in the middle. Lay a slat at one end of the supports so it overhangs the ends slightly. Attach it with two 1" brads driven into each support.

Then, attach another slat at the opposite ends of the floor. Fill in with evenly spaced slats between the front and back. Gaps should be less than ½". Set the floor deck into the cooler.

Cut the ¾ × ¾" Spanish cedar to 2¼" lengths for making the corner posts of the stackable trays. You can make all the trays (make as many as you think you'll need) all the same size. Or, you can design them so each tray is one inch shorter in length and width than the previous. This way, you can stack the trays and they will rest on the posts of the tray below.

Lay out a finger slot in one of the end pieces. The slot should be ¾" high and 2" long, with rounded ends. The top of the slot should be ¾" down from the top of the workpiece. Drill a ¾" hole at each slot end, and then connect the holes at the top and bottom by cutting with a jigsaw and a fine woodcutting blade. Sand lightly, and use this workpiece as a template for laying out the rest of the finger pulls.

Lay out the parts for each tray frame on a flat surface, with the corner posts resting on the surface. There should be a ¼" gap between the posts and the top edges of the frame. Assemble the frame by driving two 1" brass brads into the post at each side of each corner. Check with a framing square to make sure the trays are square.

Attach slats to the underside of each tray frame
to make the tray bottoms. For extra holding power, drill
small countersunk pilot holes and drive #4 × 1¼" brass
flathead screws.

A nicely made, custom stand will make your humidor look
more like a furnishing and less like picnic gear. It will also make
the humidor easier to access. We used cherry to make a 5"-tall
frame with internal dimensions slightly larger than the cooler
we used.

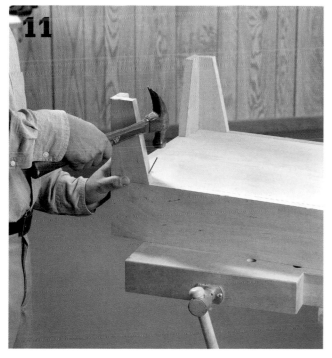

Add a support platform for the humidor and legs to the
stand, and then sand and finish it to your tastes. If you need
more assistance in designing and building a stand for your
humidor, consult a woodworking reference book or ask at
your local woodworking supply store. They're usually happy
to assist.

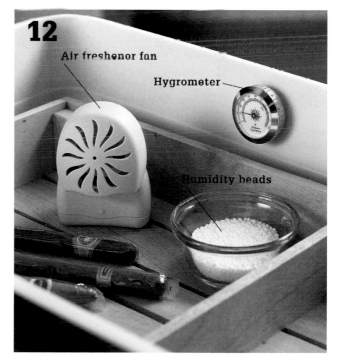

Arrange the inside of your humidor and stock it with
cigars. Try to keep the humidor at least ⅔ full at all times. Items
in the humidor should include a glass dish of cigar humidity
beads, a disposable air freshener fan (without the fragrance
package), and a hygrometer. When the hygrometer reads 68 to
70% humidity, place your cigar boxes inside the humidor.

Building a Poker Table

The top of this table is designed especially for poker, with an eight-sided playing surface and trays to hold the cups. But for those times when you just need a simple card or game table, the poker tabletop pulls off to create a small four-sided table.

Each leg pulls out easily for storage, but is held securely in place by carriage bolts and wing nuts. With the oak legs and heavy-duty construction, you can play the game without worrying about an untimely collapse – this is no flimsy, fold-down card table. The exterior components are made from oak, while the interior framework and tabletops are made from pine and birch plywood.

A removable top converts this conventional game table into a custom poker table.

Materials

(1) ¾" × 4 × 8' birch plywood
(4) 1 × 4" × 8' oak
(2) 1 × 4" × 10' pine
(2) 1 × 6" × 8' oak
(2) 2 × 2" × 6' pine
(2) ⅜ × ¹¹⁄₁₆" × 7' oak stop molding
(2) ¼ × ¾" × 7' pine shelf nosing
Wood screws
    (#6 × 1¼", #6 × 2", #6 × 2½",
    #6 × 1⅝")
1¼" brads
Wood glue
(4) ¾"-dia. × 3"-long carriage bolts
    with washers and wing nuts
(15') ¾" birch veneer edge tape
Finishing materials

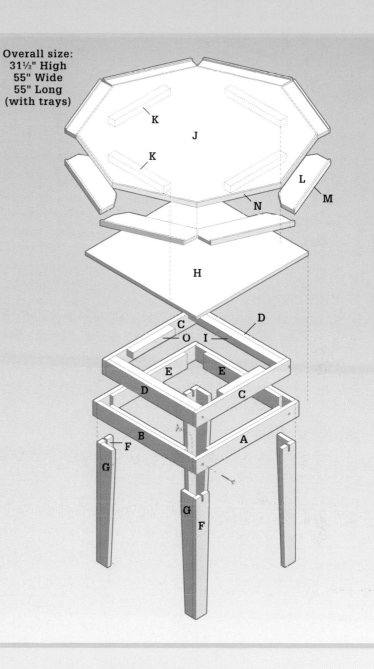

Overall size:
31½" High
55" Wide
55" Long
(with trays)

Cutting List

Key	Part	Dimension	Pcs.	Material
A	Apron side	¾ × 3½ × 30"	2	Oak
B	Apron end	¾ × 3½ × 28½"	2	Oak
C	Liner side	¾ × 3½ × 27"	2	Pine
D	Liner end	¾ × 3½ × 25½"	2	Pine
E	Filler block	¾ × 3½ × 21½"	4	Pine
F	Leg front	¾ × 3½ × 30"	4	Oak
G	Leg side	¾ × 2¾ × 30"	4	Oak
H	Main top	¾ × 32 × 32"	1	Plywood

Key	Part	Dimension	Pcs.	Material
I	Main cleat	1½ × 1½ × 25½"	2	Pine
J	Poker top	¾ × 48 × 48"	1	Plywood
K	Poker cleat	1½ × 1½ × 16"	4	Pine
L	Tray	¾ × 5½ × 18"	8	Oak
M	Tray trim	¾ × ¹¹⁄₁₆ × 18"	8	Stop molding
N	Poker trim	¼ × ¾ × *"	8	Shelf nosing
O	Short cleat	1½ × 1½ × 9"	2	Pine

*Note: Measurements reflect the actual thickness of dimensional lumber. *Cut to fit.*

How to Build a Poker Table

MAKE THE LEGS

The table legs are designed for heavy-duty support. They are tapered from the top to the bottom. Each leg is made from two 1 × 4 boards butted together. Start by cutting the leg fronts (F) and leg sides (G) to length from 1 × 4" oak. Before cutting the tapers on the leg fronts and leg sides, draw accurate cutting lines. First, designate a top and bottom to each workpiece. Mark a point on the bottoms of the leg fronts, ½" in from one long edge, then draw a mark 3½" down from the tops of the leg fronts on the same long edge. Draw a cutting line connecting the two points on the leg fronts. The leg sides are more narrow than the leg fronts. To draw the cutting lines on the leg sides, mark a point on the bottom of each leg side, 1¼" in from one long edge. Measure and mark a point 3½" down from the top and ¾" in from the same long edge. Draw cutting lines connecting the two points on the leg sides. Use a circular saw with a straightedge guide to cut along the cutting lines (photo 1). Support the leg fronts and

leg sides with a piece of scrap plywood as you cut them to size. Edge guides made from scrap and stop blocks screwed down at the ends and sides of the workpieces keep the leg parts steady as you cut them. For the most accurate results, start the taper cuts at the bottom ends. Once the leg sides and leg fronts are cut to shape, butt the untapered edges of the leg sides against the leg fronts. With the leg fronts and leg sides flush, drill evenly spaced, counterbored pilot holes through the leg fronts. Fasten the parts with glue and #6 × 1⅝" wood screws, driven through the leg fronts and into the leg sides. Fill all counterbored screw holes with ⅜"-dia. flat wood plugs. Sand the legs smooth.

MAKE THE APRON

The apron is a frame that holds the legs securely at the corners and supports the tabletops. The apron is actually a frame within a frame, made from strong, solid oak on the outside with a less expensive pine liner and filler blocks. L-shaped gaps at the corners

Use a straightedge guide and scrap-plywood stop blocks when cutting leg tapers with a circular saw.

Position the liner assembly inside the apron assembly so it fits against filler blocks.

of the apron hold the legs, which are secured with carriage bolts and wing nuts. Start by cutting the apron sides (A) and apron ends (B) to size. Position the apron ends between the apron sides with the outside faces of the apron ends flush with the ends of the apron sides. Drill counterbored pilot holes and use glue and #6 × 1⅝" wood screws to fasten the parts. Cut the liner sides (C) and liner ends (D) to size from 1 × 4" pine. Position the liner ends between the liner sides, making sure the edges are flush. Drill pilot holes, and fasten the liner ends between the liner sides with glue and #6 × 2" wood screws, driven through the liner and into the apron. Draw reference lines on the inside faces of the apron sides and apron ends, 3½" in from each corner. Cut the filler blocks (E) to size, and fasten them between the reference lines, using glue and countersunk #6 × 1¼" wood screws. With the apron on a flat surface, set the liner assembly inside the apron (photo 2), and fasten the liner assembly to the filler blocks with glue and #6 × 2" wood screws.

ATTACH THE LEGS

The legs are inserted into the gaps at the corners of the frame and secured with carriage bolts. Start by sliding the wide ends of the legs into the gaps at each corner of the apron frame. They should fit snugly, with their tops flush with the apron top. Mark the outside faces of the apron sides for carriage-bolt holes. Center the holes 3¼" in from the apron side ends. With the legs held firmly in place, drill a ⅜"-dia. hole through the apron, legs, and liner at each corner (photo 3). Remove the legs. At the top of the leg fronts, use a jigsaw to extend the holds all the way to the top of the leg fronts (photo 4). These notches allow you to remove the legs for storage without having to remove the carriage bolts. Insert the legs, and push the carriage bolts through the holes. Slide washers on the bolts, and attach wing nuts to secure the legs in place. If one or two legs do not fit precisely, try switching them around – you may find a better fit.

Hold the legs firmly, and drill ⅜"-diameter holes through the apron, legs, and liner for carriage bolts at all corners.

Cut a notch from the top of the leg fronts down to the carriage bolt hole to make it easier to remove and install legs.

(continued)

MAKE THE MAIN TOP

The main top is used as a game table and as a base for the poker tabletop. Begin by cutting the main top (H), main cleats (I), and short cleats (O) to size. Sand the parts smooth, and apply self-adhesive birch veneer edge tape to all four edges of the main top. Trim and sand the excess edge tape. Draw reference lines on one face of the main top, 2¼" in from each edge. Center the main cleats and short cleats on the main top with their outside edges on the reference lines. Fasten the cleats, making sure the main cleats are on opposite sides. Test-fit the main top on the apron. If the main top doesn't fit, realign the cleats. Fasten the main top to the liner by driving 2½" countersunk screws through the main cleats and into the liner and filler blocks (photo 5).

MAKE THE POKER TOP

The poker top is a large octagonal tabletop with ledges to hold poker ships. Cleats are attached on the bottom of the poker top so it can be centered over the main top. To cut the poker top (J) to size, start with a 48" square piece of plywood. Marking the octagonal cutting lines require a little basic geometry. First, draw reference lines between opposite corners, locating the center of the workpiece. Mark the centers of the edges on each of the four sides. Draw lines across the poker top, connecting opposing-edge centerpoints. Next, construct a homemade bar compass by drilling a centered screw hole at one end of a 1 × 2" piece of scrap. (The scrap piece must be at least 25" in length.) Drill another centered hole for a pencil, 24" up from the first hole. Drive a screw through the first hole and into the poker top centerpoint. Slip a pencil into the remaining hole, and rotate the bar compass to draw a 48"-dia. circle on the poker top. Using a straightedge, draw cutting lines connecting the points where the reference lines intersect with the circle (photo 6). Cut along the pencil lines with a circular saw, and sand the poker top to smooth out any rough edges or saw marks. To cut the poker trim (N) to fit against the poker top sides, use a power miter box or a backsaw and miter box to cut a 22½° outside bevel on one end of a

Fasten the main top to the liner by driving screws through the main cleats and short cleats and into the liner and filler blocks.

Carefully draw the cutting lines for the poker top, using a straightedge and a homemade bar compass.

poker trim piece. Note 22½° is commonly marked on miter boxes, circular saws, and radial-arm saws. After cutting this bevel, position the poker trim against one edge of the poker top. Mark the trim where the next point contacts it (photo 7), then cut another bevel that slants in the opposite direction from the bevel at the other end. Attach the trim piece to the poker top with glue and 1¼" brads, and continue cutting and measuring the poker trim to fit the table. Fill all the brad holes with wood putty and sand the edges smooth when dry.

ATTACH THE TRAYS

Trays are attached to each edge of the octagonal poker top to hold poker chips. Cut the trays and tray trim (M) to size. In order for the trays to fit on the underside of the poker top, the inside corners on one long edge on each tray are trimmed off at a 45° angle. Draw cutting lines at each end of one long edge, forming a triangle with 2"-long sides, and use a power miter box or a circular saw to cut the corners. Use glue and 1¼" brads to fasten the tray trim to the square long edge of each tray so the bottoms are flush. Turn the poker top upside down. Use glue and #6 × 1¼" wood screws to fasten the trays to the poker top at each straight edge. The trays should extend 3½" beyond the poker top edges, so use a piece of 1 × 4 as a spacer between the tray trim and the poker top edges as you fit the pieces together. Cut the poker cleats (K) to size, and position them on the poker top centerlines. (The poker cleats hold the poker top in place while it sits on the main top.) Center the poker cleats on the lines, and make sure their inside edges are 16⅛" in from the center of the table. Fasten the poker cleats with glue and #6 × 1¼" wood screws (photo 8).

APPLY FINISHING TOUCHES

Set all nail heads and fill all nail holes with untinted, stainable wood putty. Glue ⅜"-dia. oak plugs into all screw counterbores, then sand to level. Finish-sand all surfaces, and apply your finish of choice. We used three coats of tung oil.

Mark the trim pieces to fit the edges of the poker table, and cut them to length with a 22½° bevel.

Fasten the poker cleats to the underside of the poker table, 16⅛" from the center of the table.

Library Projects

Whether you're an avid reader or you simply want to give your house a culture upgrade, you probably have a very specific idea of how a library should look and feel. For some of us, a library is a rather masculine room, with a generous helping of rich wood millwork, massive formal bookcases, a sturdy wood library table, comfortable seating, and perhaps a large fireplace with a gild-framed portrait of a scowling forebearer hanging above the mantel. For others, a library may be an open, airy retreat filled with greenery, good light, and plenty of reading material to be savored over a cup of tea.

Whether the primary activity it houses is reading or entertainment, the one feature a library must have is books. Toward that end, we've provided a complete plan for a lovely floor-to-ceiling oak bookcase you can build as the centerpiece of your new library. Because a library is also about ambience, we've included two quick projects that throw a little light and charm on the room: installing a wall sconce and adding faux frame-and-panel wainscoting.

In This Chapter:

- Gallery of Home Libraries
- All About Home Libraries
- Floor-to-Ceiling Bookcase
- Library Ladder
- Rolling Ladders
- Wall Sconces
- Wainscoting
- Ceiling Beams
- Hidden Rooms

Gallery of Home Libraries

Floor-to-ceiling bookcases present decorative opportunities as well as storage solutions. Showcase an art collection or other treasured pieces along with the books.

The best libraries include plenty of places to curl up with a good book. In this library, readers can choose between a cozy window seat, a comfy, overstuffed chair, and an inviting sofa. A neutral color scheme makes the books the star of the show.

One can imagine the mysteries of the world being solved in a library such as this. The deep color of the end walls and the elaborate molding above the bookshelves lends an old-world feeling to the room.

Modular bookcases have a feeling of permanence, but unlike built-in bookcases they can be rearranged easily as your needs change. It is a good idea to anchor taller modular bookcases to a wall, however.

Controlling glare is vital to a comfortable reading environment as well as to protecting the books in your library. Choose window treatments, such as plantation shutters, that can filter the light or block it entirely, as you wish.

Floor-to-ceiling bookcases transform this wide hall into a commodious library. Shelves must be well supported to accommodate the weight of a collection such as this one.

The ultraviolet light in sunshine can cause books to become brittle and discolored and, eventually, to degrade. If your library windows have significant light exposure, fit them with room-darkening window treatments.

All About Home Libraries

Bookcases are the first and most basic requirement for a library. If you are storing new books, almost any type of material is adequate. If you're storing vintage or antique books, experts recommend glass or metal shelves. If you live in an earthquake-prone area, secure your bookcases with earthquake brackets attached to the studs behind the walls. In more contemporary library settings, you may prefer the openness of wall-mounted shelving to cabinet-style bookcases.

Floor-to-ceiling bookcases are beautiful, but the top shelves can be very difficult to reach. Enter the library ladder, a classic luxury with a practical purpose. A stationary library ladder (see pages 116 to 119) provides excellent access, and a rolling library ladder (see pages 120 to 121) adds incomparable ambience. If you've got space in your library and your budget, it would be hard to go wrong by adding a library ladder.

Book covers fade if they're left in the sun too long, so position your bookshelves out of the direct sun. On the other hand, pages and even covers mold if the books are exposed to too much moisture. Maintain the library's relative humidity level between 35 and 40 percent when the outside temperature is above 20°F. If necessary, run a humidifier to add moisture or a dehumidifier to remove it.

Ban Dirty Books ▸

Keeping books clean adds years to their lifespans because microscopic dust particles are actually quite sharp. Slip an old cotton sock onto your hand and use it to dust your books. Clean their spines with an old, soft, child-sized toothbrush.

Tip ▸

A dehumidifier is important to maintaining room humidity levels. A relative humidity level between 35 and 40% is ideal for book storage.

Treasures such as these leather-bound editions and original pieces of art find a suitable home among more contemporary books and vintage treasures. Mixing collections in this way creates interesting texture and ambience in a library.

Lighting

Lighting, including ambient, natural and general, is especially worthy of attention in a library. Ophthalmologists report that—no matter what your mother told you—reading in the dark won't make you go blind. But, they say, poor lighting forces your eye muscles to work harder, which causes eye strain and headaches. Besides, a well-lit library is simply more inviting and more comfortable.

Special color-balanced lightbulbs for reading areas reduce eye stress and make it easier to focus and concentrate. These bulbs provide glare-free light that provides natural color as in sunlight.

Light Height Tip ▶

The bottom of the shade on a reading lamp should be at shoulder height when you're seated next to it.

Quality of light is very important for reading. Look for naturally balanced lightbulbs that replicate daylight. They are available in incandescent, fluorescent, and compact fluorescent bulbs, as well as L.E.D. lights.

Floor-to-Ceiling Bookcase

Few furnishings add prestige to a space like a formal floor-to-ceiling bookcase. Typically built from clear hardwood, the classically designed bookcase delivers a refined, Old World feel. The bookcase shown here is made from red oak plywood and red oak 1× stock and moldings finished with a high gloss urethane. What's also nice about this piece is that it incorporates the wall behind it to balance all that clear hardwood with a splash of color and depth. This is a fixed-shelf design that enables you to build shelves anywhere you like to match your needs. And, because the shelf bays are built in a modular fashion, you can design it to any dimensions you wish.

The formal bookcase shown here is 8 feet long, 8 feet high and installed on a 12-foot long wall. Because it's centered in the space, the moldings and sides return to the wall, creating niches on the left and right that are great for decoration. However, this bookcase can be built wall-to-wall if desired. It's a flexible design. Finally, the exact same style shelf can be built to take paint. Instead of using red oak, though, poplar is a great choice.

Built-ins offer a sense of quality craftsmanship that is built to last. The crown molding, rosettes, and fluted molding all speak to the luxury of having fine bookshelves in your home.

Tools

Miter saw
Table saw
Circular saw
Router
Drill/Driver
Level
Stud finder
Pull saw
Flat bar
Stepladder or
    work platform
Air nailer
Combination square
Drywall or
    deck screws
Finish nails
Glue
Finishing materials

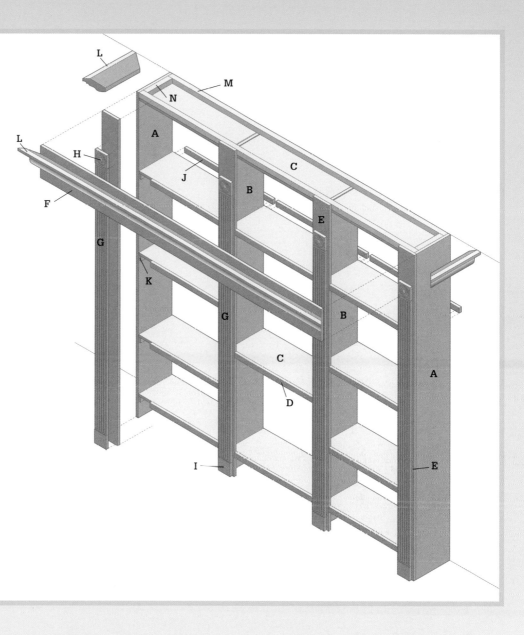

Materials

(3) ¾" × 4 × 8 red oak plywood
(11) 1 × 2 × 96" red oak
(4) 1 × 6 × 96" red oak
(1) 1 × 10 × 96" red oak
(4) ⅝" × 3⅜ × 84" fluted oak molding
(4) Rosettes
(4) Plinth blocks
12 lineal ft. red oak crown molding
(3) 2 × 2 × 96" pine

Cutting List

Part	No.	Desc.	Size	Material
A	2	Upright (outer)	¾ × 11½ × 96"	Red oak plywood
B	2	Upright (inner)	¾ × 11½ × 94½"	Red oak plywood
C	14	Shelf	¾ × 11½ × 31"	Red oak plywood
D	11	Shelf nosing	¾ × 1½ × 31"	Red oak 1 × 2
E	4	Upright backer	¾ × 5½ × 96"	Red oak 1 × 6
F	1	Fascia	¾ × 9½ × 96"	Red oak 1 × 10
G	4	Fluted molding	⅝ × 3⅜ × 78½"	Red oak molding

Part	No.	Desc.	Size	Material
H	4	Rosette	¾ × 4 × 4"	Red oak molding
I	4	Plinth block	¾ × 4 × 4"	Red oak molding
J	11	Shelf cleat (wall)	¾ × 1½ × 31"	Red oak 1 × 2
K	22	Shelf cleat (side)	¾ × 1½ × 10¾"	Red oak 1 × 2
L	3	Crown molding	½ × 3³⁄₁₆" × cut to fit	Red oak molding
M	2	Ceiling cleat (long)	1½ × 1½ × 94½"	2 × 2
N	2	Ceiling cleat (short)	1½ × 1½ × 8½"	2 × 2

How to Build a Floor-to-Ceiling Bookcase

Cut through the base molding at the edges of the project area and remove it so the bookcase can fit tightly up against the wall.

Carefully mark out the plumb lines for the outside edges of the uprights and continue the mark up onto the ceiling.

Use a spacer as a gauge for marking the position of the front edge of the 2 × 2 nailing frame that is attached to the ceiling.

LAY OUT THE PROJECT ON YOUR WALL

This bookcase is designed to be built at your installation site. The best place to begin is by drawing layout lines on the wall. The most important lines mark the locations of the four uprights, which need to be vertical and parallel, and the shelf cleats that must be horizontal and parallel. Start by locating the centerline for the bookcase installation and marking it on the baseboard and on the wall. Measure out 4 feet on each side of the centerline and make marks for the outside edges of the bookcase. These lines denote the outer faces of the left and right uprights. Using a pull saw (if you have one), cut and remove the baseboard between the left and right marks. Make your cuts as square as possible (photo 1).

Measure and make a mark 15⅞" on each side of the centerline, dividing the project area into three equal bays. On each side of all three vertical lines, mark out ⅜" to establish the locations of the ¾"-thick uprights.

Measuring up from the floor, mark horizontal shelf cleat locations on the walls at the back of each bay. The cleats should stop at the upright locations so the ¾"-thick uprights can fit snugly in between the cleat ends. In the drawing, there is one bottom shelf, set 6½" off the floor in all three bays. The left and right bays have shelves 24", 48", and 72" up from the floor. The center bay has a single center shelf set at 36" off the top of the bottom shelf ledger and a top shelf at 72". Using a 4-ft. level, mark horizontal reference lines for the shelf cleats in all three bays. Draw a small "X" below each line as a reminder of which side of the line to fasten the cleat. Then, use the 4-ft. level to extend the outlines for the uprights all the way up from the floor to the ceiling (photo 2). These sets of parallel lines should be ¾" apart and plumb.

At the ceiling, lay out the location for the 2 × 2 frame that creates nailing surfaces for the outer uprights and the 1 × 6 upright backers that are centered on the front edges of the uprights. The 2 × 2 frame should span from the inside faces of the outer uprights and extend 11½" out from the wall (photo 3).

> ## Tip ▸
>
> Make an 11½"-wide spacer to use as a marking gauge.

4

Attach the 2 × 2 nailing frame to the ceiling at the layout lines, making sure to catch a ceiling joist where possible and using appropriate anchors in spots where no joist is present.

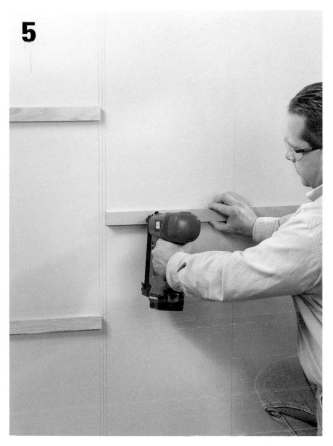

5

Attach all of the shelf cleats to the wall, making sure to preserve an even ¾" gap between cleat ends to make room for the inner uprights.

If you're installing undercabinet lights, such as puck lights, locate the center of each bay on the ceiling and mark them for lights. Get a qualified electrician to install the wiring, fixtures, and switches. If you're doing the work yourself, follow local building codes. Pull the wire through the drywall or plaster and pigtail (curl up) for fixture installation later.

INSTALL THE NAILING FRAME

For ease of installation, assemble the 2 × 2 nailing frame on the ground. Use 2½" pneumatic finish nails or wallboard screws to join the 2 × 2 frame components. Test to make sure the assembly is square. Attach the frame to the ceiling by screwing up through the members at the ceiling joist locations; use an electronic stud finder to identify these (photo 4). Attach the frame to the wall's top plate at the wall/ceiling joint. If the ceiling joists are parallel to the

wall, you may need to use toggle bolts or other wall anchors to secure the frame along the front edge.

ATTACH THE SHELF CLEATS TO THE WALL

While plenty of fasteners, including trim head wood screws or 8d nails, may be dependably used to connect the 1 × 2 red oak shelf cleats to the walls at stud locations, a pneumatic or cordless finish nailer loaded with 2" nails is ideal for the task. It eliminates the need to pre-drill and countersink fasteners, as you would when driving screws or hand-nailing into hardwood. A pneumatic nailer also dispenses fasteners quickly and accurately, making it much easier when you're working alone. Cut and install the cleats (J) at the layout lines. A few dabs of construction adhesive applied to the wall behind the cleats will add even more strength to the connection. Fasten the cleats so the upright panels can be installed around them (photo 5).

(continued)

INSTALL THE UPRIGHTS

Cut the outer uprights (A) to full room height in length. Rest the bottoms on the floor and nail the top ends to the ends of the 2 × 2 nailing frame (photo 6). Also drive 8d finish nails through the uprights and into the ends of the shelf cleats in the outer bays (drill pilot holes first).

Rout a roundover, bead, or chamfer onto each edge of the upright backer (E), if desired (photo 7). Cut the inner uprights (B) (11½" wide) to length. They should be 1½" shorter than the outer uprights because they butt up against the underside of the 2 × 2 nailing frame on the ceiling. Position the inner uprights between the ends of the shelf cleats that are attached to the wall in each bay. At the ceiling, use a framing square to make sure the inner uprights are perpendicular to the wall and then position a 1 × 6 upright backer over the upright edge. Center the backer on the upright edge and nail it to the 2 × 2 nailing frame. Double-check that the upright is perpendicular to the wall by measuring the bays at the wall and at the front of the upright and making sure the measurements are the same. Then drill pilot holes and drive 8d finish nails (or pneumatic nails) through the backer and into the edge of the upright at 12" intervals (photo 8). Install both inner uprights.

INSTALL THE SHELVES

The shelves and shelf cleats help solidify the structure, so install them next. Start by nailing a shelf (C) to the 2 × 2 ceiling frame at the top of each bay (photo 9).

Nail the outer uprights to the ends of the nailing frame attached to the ceiling.

Routing a bead, roundover, or chamfer adds nice detail and shadow lines to the upright backers.

Attach the upright backers to the front edges of the inner uprights with pneumatic or hand-driven finish nails.

Attach a shelf at the top of each bay to conceal the framework attached to the ceiling.

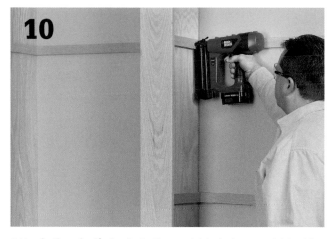

Attach the shelf cleats to the uprights, being careful to drive fasteners straight to prevent damage to the upright panels.

Edge the red oak shelves with 1 × 2 red oak nosing that's bonded to the shelves with glue and finish nails.

Conceal the gap between the top of the bookcase and ceiling with crown molding or sprung cove molding. Installing crown molding can get complicated. Consult a trim carpentry book if you are unsure how to work with crown molding.

Attach the plinth blocks, rosettes, and fluted case moldings to complete the trimwork installation.

Attach the short shelf cleats (K) to the sides of the uprights so each shelf is supported on three sides (photo 10). Use a level to make sure the cleats are level, and attach them with 4d finish nails or 1⅜" brads and adhesive.

Cut the remaining shelves (C) to length and set them on the cleats. Cut the 1 × 2 shelf nosing (D) and attach it to the front edges of the exposed shelves, making sure the shelves are flush with the top edge of the nosing (photo 11). Use 4d finish nails driven through pilot holes or pneumatic finish nails to attach the nosing.

ATTACH THE TRIM

Cut the 1 × 10 red oak fascia board (F) the full width of the bookcase and nail it to the top so the ends are flush

with the outer faces of the outer uprights. Make sure the fascia board is level before attaching it with nails driven into the tops of the upright backers. Once the fascia board is in place, cut, fit, and attach the crown molding (L) and molding return at the top (photo 12).

Install the plinth blocks (I) at the bottom of each upright backer, resting on the floor and centered side to side. Then, attach the rosettes (H) at the top of each upright backer, centered side to side. Measure from the bottom of the rosette to the top of the plinth block and cut the fluted case molding (G) to fit. Install with adhesive and nails (photo 13). Fill nail holes, sand, and apply finish. If the installation room has base shoe moldings, you may want to add them to your bookcase for a consistent look.

Library Ladder

Floor-to-ceiling bookcases will cease to be unreachable and changing lightbulbs in your ceiling fixtures will be less threatening once you've built this charming library ladder. Offering all the safety and convenience of a stepladder, this three-step, rung-style ladder surpasses just about any store-bought climbing structure in style and design. When extended, the runged stepladder sides provide sturdy support of the ladder treads.

When not in use, the ladder folds together so it can be stored up against a wall and out of the traffic flow.

Designed for efficiency in use and in construction, this oak stepladder can be built with only three 8-foot-long 1 × 4 boards and a few feet of oak doweling. The treads are fastened to the sides of the ladder with oak through dowels for long-lasting joints that stand up to repeated use.

Safety Notice ▶

When using any ladder, always exercise good judgment and safety practices. Make sure the legs of the ladder are firmly planted on a level floor before use. Do not use the dowel rungs as steps. Do not carry heavy objects while using the ladder. This ladder is suitable for light-duty, indoor use only.

This 3-step library ladder will grant access to upper shelves to any average-height person. When not in use, it can be folded up for flat storage.

Materials

(3) 1 × 4" × 8' red oak
(2) 1"-dia. × 4' oak dowel
(1) ⅜"-dia. × 4' oak dowel
4d finish nails
Wood glue
(2) 10" chest lid supports
Finishing materials

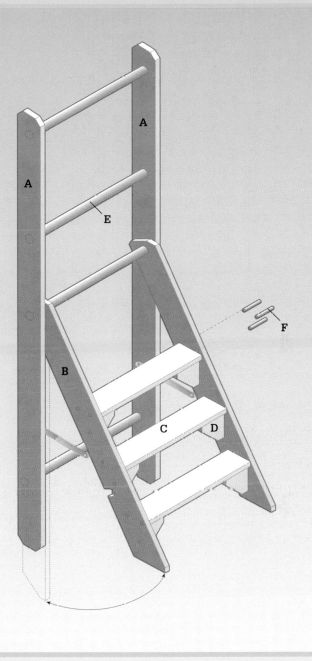

Overall Size:
58½" High
19⅜" Wide
25¼" Deep

Cutting List

Key	Part	Dimension	Pcs.	Material
A	Ladder side	¾ × 3½ × 58½"	2	Red oak
B	Step rail	¾ × 3½ × 40¼"	2	Red oak
C	Step tread	¾ × 3½ × 15½"	3	Red oak
D	Tread brace	¾ × 3½ × 3½"	6	Red oak
E	Cross dowel	1"-dia. × 19⅜"	4	Oak dowel
F	Through dowel	⅜"-dia. × 2"	18	Oak dowel

Note: Measurements reflect the actual thickness of dimensional lumber.

How to Make a Library Ladder

MAKE THE LADDER STEPS

The steps for the library ladder consist of flat treads with triangular braces on each end. They are assembled first, then attached to the ladder sides with oak through dowels. Cut the step treads (C) to length from 1 × 4 oak, then cut the tread braces (D) to 3½" square. Mark points 2½" in from one of the corners of each tread brace, then connect the points to make cutting lines. For maximum brace strength, mark the cutting lines so the wood grain in each brace runs vertically when the brace is installed. Make the cutoffs with a jigsaw or miter saw, then sand the edges smooth. Attach a brace to each end of each tread (photo 1), so the outer face of each brace is recessed ½" from the front edge of the tread. Use glue and 4d finish nails driven through pilot holes to attach the treads.

MAKE THE STEP RAILS

The step rails support the ladder treads. They are trimmed at one end so they lie flat on the floor when the ladder is set up. Each rail also contains a U-shaped cutout to fit over the bottom rung on the ladder sides. Cut the step rails (B) to length from 1 × 4 red oak. Mark points ¾" in from each corner on one end of each rail, then connect the points to make cutting lines for the triangular cutoffs at the top ends of the rails. Make the cutoffs with a jigsaw. On the square end of one rail (this will be the bottom), mark points ⅝" in from one corner, in each direction.

Mark another point on the edge, 2" up from the opposite corner. Connect the 2" point to the mark on the bottom to make a 35° cutoff line, then cut with a jigsaw or miter saw. Sand the cut smooth, then use the first rail as a template for tracing a matching cutoff onto the other rail. This helps ensure that the legs will be uniform in shape. Cut and sand the second cutoff. Now, mark reference lines for positioning the tread assemblies onto the rails. Measuring up from the bottom, mark points on the shorter edge of each rail at 7½", 15½", and 21½". Set a T-bevel (if you have one) to match the angle on the bottoms of the rails, then use the T-bevel to extend reference lines out from the reference points on the rails. The reference lines should be parallel to the bottoms of the rails (photo 2). If you don't own a T-bevel, set a 1 × 4 scrap onto one of the rails so the edges are flush and the scrap extends slightly past the bottom end. Trace the bottom cut onto the scrap, extending the line so it runs straight across the scrap board. Cut along the cutting line, then use the 1 × 4 as a guide for tracing the correct angle onto the rails.

ASSEMBLE THE TREADS & RAILS

Attach the tread assemblies between the rails at the reference lines, using glue and clamps. The fronts of the treads should be flush with the front edges of the rails, with the tops flush up against the reference lines on the rails. When the glue has dried, carefully unclamp

Attach the tread braces recessed ½" from the front edge of the tread and flush with the end.

Draw reference lines for positioning the treads parallel to the bottoms of the step rails.

the assembly, then drill three ⅜"-dia. × 1½"-deep dowel holes through the rails and into the tread assemblies at each joint. Two of the holes should extend into the end of the tread, and one should extend into the brace. Cut eighteen 2"-long dowel rods (E) from ⅜"-dia. oak doweling (or use ⅜"-dia. dowel pins). Make sure the guide holes are free of sawdust, then apply glue to the ends of each dowel and insert them into the dowel holes. Drive the dowels all the way into the dowel holes with a wooden mallet, being careful not to break the glue bonds at the joints (photo 3). Use a saw to trim the ends of the dowels so they are nearly flush with the rails, then sand the ends flush.

Make the ladder sides. Cut the ladder sides (A) to length. Mark and cut triangular cutoffs with ¾" legs at each corner of each end. Drill 1"-dia. holes through the sides at points centered (edge to edge) at 31", 41½", and 55½" up from the bottoms of the sides. Mark another centerpoint 1¼" in from the back edge of each side, 7½" up from each bottom. To ensure that these 1"-dia. guide holes for the ladder rungs are aligned, clamp the sides together with all edges and ends flush, and drill through both boards at the same time.

JOIN THE RAILS & LADDER SIDES

The rail/tread assembly is attached to the ladder sides with a 1"-dia. dowel rung (F) that passes through the tops of the rails and is seated in the lowest centered holes in the ladder sides. Drill 1⅛"-dia. guide holes at the top of each stop rail, centered from edge to edge and with centerpoints that are 1½" down from the top ends. Set the step assembly between the ladder sides so the holes are aligned with the lowest centered hole in each ladder side. Drive a 1" dowel (F) through all four holes, then slip the ends of the dowel out of the sides in turn, apply glue inside the guide holes in the sides, then reinsert the ends of the dowel. Drill pilot holes, then drive a 4d finish nail through an edge of each ladder side and into the ends of the dowel (this keeps the dowel from spinning). Also install 1"-dia. dowels (F) in the top two holes. Position the ladder so the rails are flush with the edges of the ladder sides, and trace the lowest holds in the sides onto the outer faces of the rails. Swing the ladder and sides apart, then drill 1¼" dia. holes through the rails. Draw lines perpendicular to the back edges of the rails, connected to the top and bottom of the hole in each rail. Cut along the lines with a jigsaw to make the notches (photo 4) so the rails will lock over the bottom rung when closed. Install a 1" dowel (F) in the bottom holes in the ladder sides. Install a chest lid support about midway up from the bottom of each rail, then attach the free ends of the ladder sides so the lid support locks into position when the ladder is set up (make sure the ends of the rails and sides all are flush against the floor). Finish-sand the exposed surfaces, then apply your finish of choice. We left the wood natural and applied three coats of water-based polyurethane.

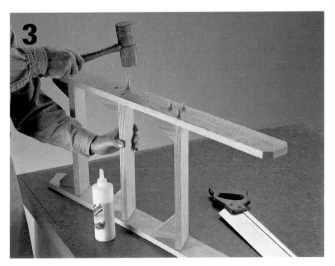

Drive three glued, 2"-long dowels into each step tread joint after the glue in the joints has set.

Cut U-shaped notches in the back edges of the step rails so they will lock over the bottom dowel rung.

Rolling Ladders

Rolling library ladders conjure images of elegance, of wealth and graceful living. Most people have never seen one outside of old movies and the board game *Clue*. Think how impressed friends and family would be to find one in your home.

Installing a rolling ladder is not as complicated as you might think. The key to the project is taking accurate measurements and then purchasing a ladder specifically suited to your application. Many suppliers offer detailed instructions for measuring the space, ordering the correct parts, and installing their products.

Fixed Library Ladders Tip ▶

The classic library ladder is the rolling variety, with a track or rail near the ceiling for the tops of the legs and wheels at the bottoms of the legs. For a number of reasons, not the least of which is product liability insurance costs, rolling ladders are rather expensive. One way to save a bit of money is to purchase a hardware kit from a woodworker's catalog or store and then build your own ladder. Or, you may choose to sacrifice the convenience of rolling and employ a fixed ladder instead to reach your upper shelves. Some furniture stores carry 6- or 7-ft., non-rolling library ladders that hook onto a track or are rail-mounted near the top of a bookcase. To move the ladder you simply lift it, carry it, or slide it and re-hook it. It's not as elegant, but this type of ladder can be purchased for a fraction of the cost of a rolling ladder.

Library ladders provide easy access to high shelves, but their contributions go well beyond that: they instill mystery and romance into even the most practical of libraries.

Many rolling ladders are designed to save space. They can be pulled out for use and then pushed back against the shelves until they're needed again.

When shopping for a library ladder, look for non-marring wheels that won't damage flooring, even hardwood floors.

Wall Sconces

Wall sconces help create an interesting, varied lighting plan that's particularly appropriate in a home library. If the walls are open to the studs during building or remodeling, installing a wall sconce is no more difficult than installing a standard light fixture. In fact, it may be easier because wall sconces are typically installed 60" above the floor, well within reach without a ladder.

All is not lost, however, if you're working with finished walls. By removing a channel of drywall, you can easily tap into an existing receptacle as a power source. This project is not difficult, but it does require

A wall sconce provides soft, subtle light in a reading area or library. If you have experience with wiring, you can complete a project like this in a weekend.

several different skill sets—wiring, drywall repair, and painting.

Ceramic sconces, like the ones shown in this project, are opaque, which means your eyes are not directly exposed to the lightbulbs. In most of these fixtures, this means you can safely use a higher wattage lightbulb: up to 150 watts incandescent or 42 watts compact fluorescent in some. When controlled with a dimmer switch, these sconces can be turned down to create soft, romantic light or turned up to provide bright task lighting.

Note: Before beginning this project, check with your municipal building department to find out if a permit and inspection are required.

Tools & Materials ▸

Electronic stud finder	Plastic switch box
Utility knife	Electrical box
Straightedge	Adjustable brace bar
Hammer	Cable clamps
Screwdriver	Single-pole
Drill/driver	dimmer switch
Circuit tester	Drywall
Cable ripper	Drywall screws
Wall sconce	Joint compound
12- or 14-gauge	
3-wire NM cable	

How to Install a Wall Sconce

Locate a receptacle near the planned location for the sconce. At your main service panel, shut off power to that receptacle. Use an electronic circuit tester or a multi-meter to test the receptacle and make sure the power is off.

Remove the face plate that covers the receptacle and then unscrew the mounting screws that fasten the receptacle to the electrical box. Disconnect the receptacle from the wiring.

Locate and mark the wall studs in the work area. Mark the fixture location (usually 60" above the floor). If the receptacle is directly beneath the sconce location (in the same stud bay), you'll want to remove all of the wallboard covering the stud bay between the sconce and the floor. Mark a cutting line 6" above the sconce location. Mark vertical cutting lines on the wallboard, centered on the wall studs that frame the bay. Remove base trim and remove the wallboard.

(continued)

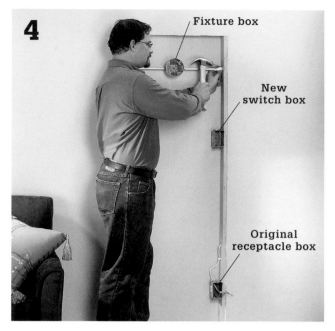

Attach a single-gang electrical box to the wall stud directly above the receptacle. Typically, the top of the box is 48" above the floor. Also attach a square or octagonal electrical fixture box to the wall stud at the sconce location. If you are installing the sconce at 60", that means the new boxes will be only 12" apart. The boxes should be positioned so the front edges will be flush with the finished wall surface after it is installed.

Run the new NM cable from the receptacle box to the switch box and from the switch box to the fixture box. Drive cable staples to secure the cable no more than 8" from each box. Strip 8" of sheathing from each cable end and ½" of insulation from each wire end. Use cable clamps.

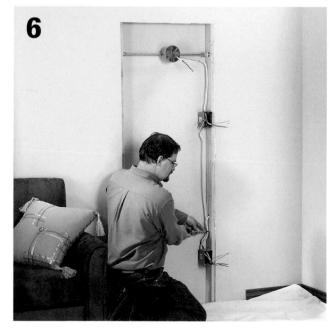

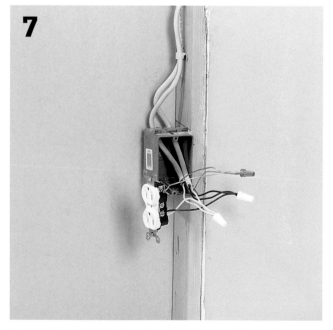

Strip about 8" of cable sheathing from the new NM cable, using a cable ripper. Then, strip ½" of insulation from the black and white wires. Remove a knockout from the top of the receptacle box and install a cable clamp. Feed the new NM cable into the receptacle box. Tighten the clamp onto the cable.

Cut 6"-long pigtail wires (two black, two white, two bare copper) and strip ½" of insulation off all ends. Twist the white wires together (including the pigtail) and secure with a wire cap. Twist together the black wire from the new NM cable, one of the black wires that was connected to the receptacle, and the black pigtail. Secure with a wire cap. Twist all bare ground wires together and secure with a green wire cap.

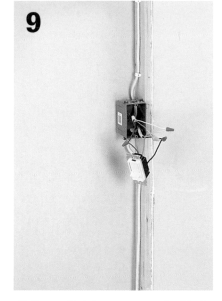

Reconnect the loose black wire to one terminal of the receptacle and connect the free end of the black pigtail to the other receptacle terminal. Pigtail the grounding wires to the grounding screw in the receptacle box. Test to make sure all connections are strong and then carefully replace the receptacle. If the wires will not fit comfortably in the box behind the receptacle, you'll need to undo the connections and replace the box with a larger one. Reattach the mounting screws to secure the receptacle to the box

At the switch box, connect the black wire from the receptacle to one terminal on the switch. Connect the black wire leading to the light to the other terminal. Connect the two white wires with a wire cap (only the black wires are connected to the switch). Connect the grounding wire to the grounding lead, if there is one. Otherwise, twist the bare ground wires together. Attach the switch to the electrical box with the mounting screws.

Patch the hole in the wall before installing the light fixture. Before patching the wall, cap the loose wire ends and tuck them safely into the fixture box. Cut a 2 × 4 nailer to fit at the top of the wall opening and screw it to the wall studs so it will back both the old and new wallboard. Cut a piece of wallboard the same thickness as the existing wall and screw it to the studs and nailer with wallboard screws. It's okay if there are small gaps around the patch.

Fill gaps around the wallboard patch and cover the recessed wallboard screw heads with joint compound. Let the compound dry, and then sand it so it is even with the surrounding wall surface. Paint to match the surrounding wall.

At the fixture box, connect the white, black, and ground wires to the light fixture as directed by the fixture installation instructions. Fasten the sconce to the fixture box with mounting screws and test.

Wainscoting

Frame-and-panel wainscot adds depth, character, and a sense of Old-World charm to any room. Classic wainscot was built with grooved or rabbeted rails and stiles that captured a floating hardwood panel. In the project shown here, the classic appearance is mimicked, but the difficulties of machining precise parts and commanding craftsman-level joinery are eliminated. Paint-grade materials (mostly MDF) are used in the project shown; however, you can also build the project with solid hardwoods and finish-grade plywood if you prefer a clear-coat finish.

Installing wainscot frames that look like frame-and-panel wainscot can be done piece by piece, but it is often easier to assemble the main frame parts in your shop. Not only does working in the shop allow you to join the frame parts together (we use pocket screws driven in the backs of the rails and stiles), it generally results in a more professional look.

Once the main frames are assembled, they can be attached to the wall at stud locations. If you prefer to site-build the wainscot piece by piece, you may need to replace the wallcovering material with plywood to create nailing surfaces for the individual frame pieces.

We primed all of the wainscot parts prior to installing them and then painted the wainscot (including the wall sections within the wainscot panel frames) a contrasting color from the wall above the wainscot cap.

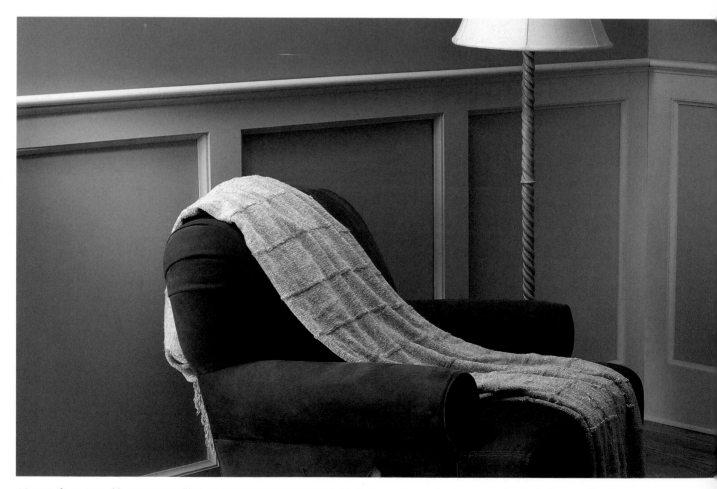

At one time, grand homes were "finished" by highly skilled trim carpenters who worked on some projects for months. Today, contemporary construction methods let you produce the Old World look of frame-and-panel wainscot without an Old World style craftsman on staff.

Tools & Materials ▸

Laser level
Pencil
Tape measure
Circular saw
  or table saw
Straightedge guide
Power miter saw
Drill with bits
Carpenter's square
Pocket hole jig
  with screws
Pry bar
Hammer

Pneumatic finish
  nail gun
  with compressor
Caulking gun
¾"-thick MDF
  sheet stock
$^{11}\!/_{16}$" cove molding
½ × ¾" base shoe
$^9\!/_{16} × 1\frac{1}{8}$"
  cap molding
  (10 ft. per panel)
Panel adhesive
Paint and primer

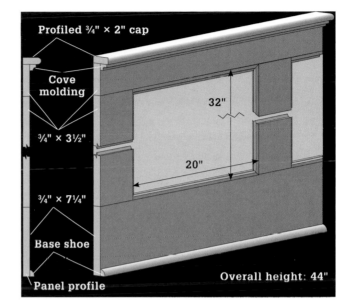

Profiled ¾" × 2" cap

Cove molding

¾" × 3½"

32"

20"

¾" × 7¼"

Base shoe

Panel profile

Overall height: 44"

How to Install Wainscot Frames

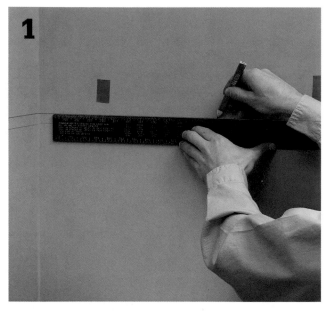

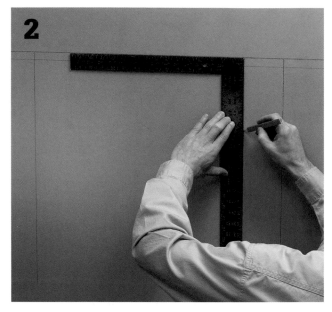

Use a laser level and a pencil to mark the height of the wainscot installation directly onto all walls in the project area. Also mark the height of the top rail (¾" below the overall height), since the cap rail will be installed after the rest of the wainscot is installed. Mark stud locations, using an electronic stud finder.

Plot out the wainscot layout on paper and then test the layout by drawing lines on the wall to make sure you're happy with the design. Try to use a panel width that can be divided evenly into all project wall lengths. In some cases, you may need to make the panel widths slightly different from wall to wall, but make sure to maintain a consistent width within each wall's run.

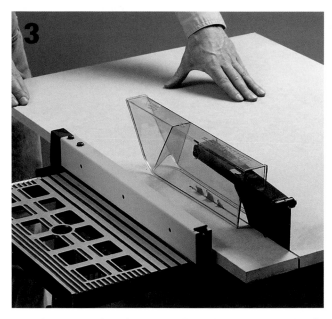

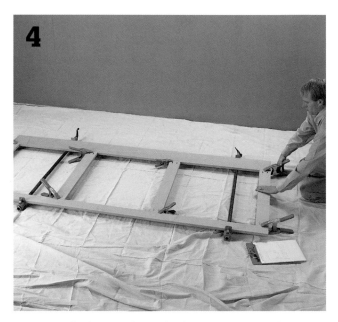

Based on your plan, rip a sheet of MDF into strips to make all of the wainscot parts except the trim moldings. In our case, that included the cap rail (2" wide), the top rail and stiles (3½" wide), and the base rail (7¼" wide). *Note: These are standard lumber dimensions. You can use 1 × 4 and 1 × 8 dimensional lumber for the rails and stiles (use 1 × 2 or rip stock for the cap rail).*

Cut top rails, base rails, and stiles (but not cap rails) to length and dry-assemble the parts into ladder frames based on your layout. Plan the layouts so wall sections longer than 8 ft. are cut with scarf joints in the rails meeting at a stud location. Dry-assemble the pieces on a flat work surface.

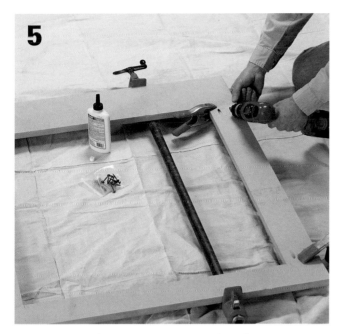

Assemble the frames using glue and pocket screws
or biscuits. Clamp the parts together first and check with a
carpenter's square to make sure the stiles are perpendicular to
both rails.

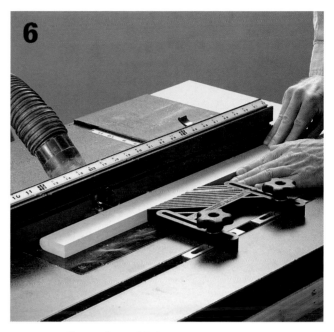

Mount a ¾" roundover bit in your router or router table
and shape a bullnose profile on the front edge of your cap
rail stock.

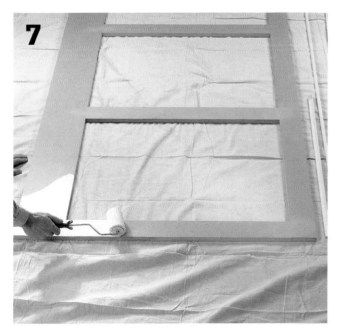

Prime all parts on both sides, including the milled moldings
and uncut cap rail stock.

Position the frames against the wall and shim underneath
the bottom rails as necessary to bring them flush with the
top rail marks on the wall (¾" below the overall height lines).
Attach the wainscot sections by driving 3" drywall screws,
countersunk, through the top rail and the bottom rail at each
stud location. If you are using scarf joints, be sure to install the
open half first.

(continued)

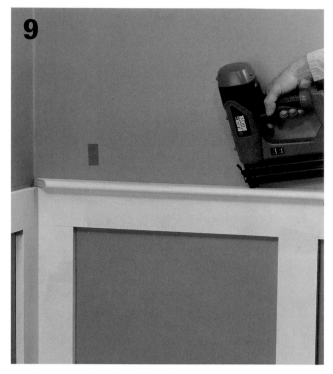

9

Cut the cap rail to length and attach it to the top rail with panel adhesive and finish nails. Toenail a 3" drywall screw through the cap rail and into the wall at each stud location. Be sure to carefully drill pilot holes and countersink holes for each screw. Miter-cut the cap rails at the corners.

10

Install cove molding in the crotch where the cap rail and top rails meet, using glue and a brad nailer. Then, nail base shoe to conceal any gaps between the bottom rails and the floor. Miter all corners.

11

Cut mitered frames to fit around the perimeter of each panel frame created by the rails and stiles. Use cap molding.

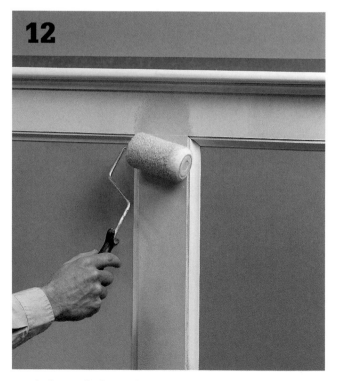

12

Mask the wall above the cap rail and then prime and paint the wainscot frames. Generally, a lighter, contrasting color than the wall color above is most effective visually.

Snap a level line at the top rail height. Because the rails and stiles are the same thickness, the backer panel should run all the way from the floor to just shy of the top of the top rail. Cut the backers so the grain will run vertically when installed. Attach them to the walls with panel adhesive, notching to fit around obstructions, such as this window opening.

Install the baseboard and top rail directly over the backer panels, using a finish nailer or by hand-nailing with 6d finish nails. The top edge of the top rail pieces should be slightly higher than the backer panels. Use your reference line as a guide for the top rail, but double-check with a level.

Attach the cap rail pieces with a finish nailer. The caps should butt flush against the wall, concealing the top edges of the backer panels. Also butt the cap rails against the window and door casings.

Cut the stile to fit between the top rail and the baseboard and install them. It's okay to vary the spacing slightly from wall to wall, but try to keep them evenly spaced on each wall. Where the wainscot meets door or window casing, butt the edges of the stiles against the casing. This can mean notching around window aprons or horns as well as door plinth blocks.

Add decorative touches, such as the corbels we cut for this installation. The corbels provide some support for the cap rail but their function is primarily decorative. We glued and nailed one corbel at each end of each cap rail piece and above each stile, and then added an intermediate one between each pair of stiles.

Ceiling Beams

Installing ceiling beams adds depth and visual appeal to vaulted or high ceilings, or even regular 8-foot ceilings that are a bit on the bland side. The beams of this project are purely decorative, but meant to suggest the heavy-duty structural members of timber-frame construction. Choose a higher-grade lumber for a cleaner look or a lower grade for a more rustic approach. The species of wood you use to build the beams may match your existing trimwork, although clear-coated hardwood beams will be more expensive than their paint-grade counterparts.

Whenever possible, install ceiling beams with fasteners driven into blocking or joists. Installation of ceiling beams is not recommended without solid backing. Standard wallboard construction is not built to hold the weight of this project with hollow wall fasteners and construction adhesive alone. Use hollow wall fasteners only when absolutely necessary.

Tools & Materials ▸

Pencil
Tape measure
Circular saw with
    straightedge guide
Power miter saw
Drill with bits
Pneumatic
    finish-nail gun
    and compressor
Caulk gun
Combination square
Painter's tape
Chalk line

1 × 6 and
    1 × 4 boards
2 × 6 framing
    lumber
Cove moldings
3" Wallboard screws
Construction
    adhesive
Hollow
    wall fasteners
1¼" pneumatic
    finish nails
Wood glue

Exposed beams lend a feeling of strength and structure to a room, even if they're really just hollow shells like the beams seen here. Because they can be attached directly to the ceiling surface, installing decorative beams is a relatively easy trim carpentry project (as long as you're comfortable working at heights).

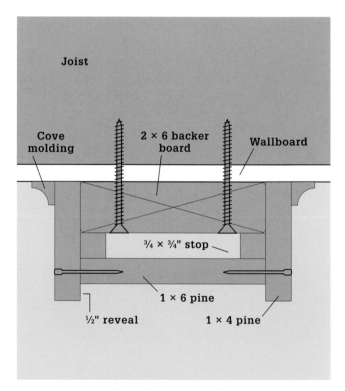

A cross-section view of the exposed beams shown being installed here reveals that they are hollow inside and actually quite simple in structure. You can install beams in any direction, but perpendicular to the ceiling joists (as shown above) is the easier orientation to work with.

How to Install Ceiling Beams

Plan the approximate location of each ceiling beam and locate the ceiling joists in the desired areas with a stud finder. Mark the joists on the ceiling with tape.

Mark the end of each joist at the point where the ceiling meets the wall. If you will be installing the beams parallel to the joists, as shown here, measure out from the center of each joist one-half the width of the backer board you'll be installing (2¾" for a 2 × 6) and make a reference mark. Make reference marks at the same relative spots where the opposite wall meets the ceiling. For installations parallel to the joists, offsetting the marks results in visible reference lines for the edges of the backer boards.

Use a chalk line to snap straight reference lines across the ceiling. Have a helper hold the line on the corresponding reference mark. If you are installing the beams perpendicular to the joists, you may want to avoid snapping a chalk line, since marking chalk (especially red chalk) is hard to remove and can even telegraph through paint. An option that won't mark up the ceiling is to string a grid of unchalked lines across the ceiling to mark the positions of the beams and the locations of the joists. Then, mark an X at every point where the lines intersect and remove the lines before installing the backer boards for the beams.

(continued)

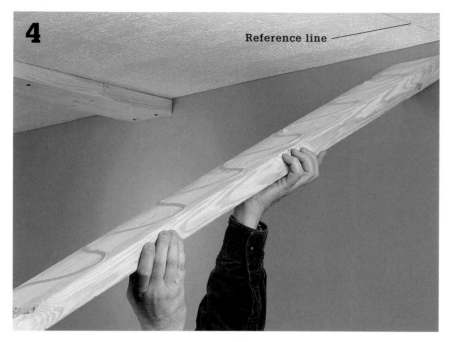

Reference line

Measure, cut, and install 2 × 6 backer boards according to your reference lines. Use construction adhesive to adhere the blocking to the ceiling and drive 3" wallboard screws through the blocking and into the joists. *Tip: If you're working alone, drive a few screws into the backers (preferably at known joist locations) before you position it. Then, you can hold the board in place with one hand and drive the screws with the other hand. A better plan, of course, is to recruit a helper.*

Option: In areas where a ceiling joist is not available and blocking is difficult to install, use hollow wall fasteners (such as the toggle bolt shown here) to install the backers. At the end of each backer you can toenail 3" screws into the top plate of the wall to provide additional support.

Set the blade of a combination square to 1¼" and mark the back face of the 1 × 4 beam sides with a pencil. Slide the square along the edge of the piece and hold the tip of the pencil against the end of the blade. Mark enough stock for each beam side.

Use a table saw (best tool) or a circular saw and a straightedge guide to cut ¾ × ¾" strips off of 1× pine for the stop molding. Cut enough stock to apply to each beam side piece.

Align the stop-molding strips with the reference marks on the beam sides. Nail and glue the ¾" strips to the back faces of the beam sides with 1¼" finish nails and wood glue.

Cut the side pieces to length with a power miter saw, using scarf joints to join each piece that is more than 8 feet long. Butt the ends of the beams into the opposing walls, making sure the joints are tight. Nail the sides in place using 1½" finish nails driven every 12" into the blocking.

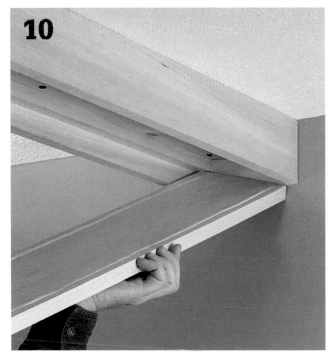

Install the bottom pieces of the beams with wood glue and 1½" nails driven into the ¾" strips on the inside of the beams. Make sure the ends butt into the walls snugly, and use scarf joints where joining pieces together (offset the scarf joints from seams in the beam sides).

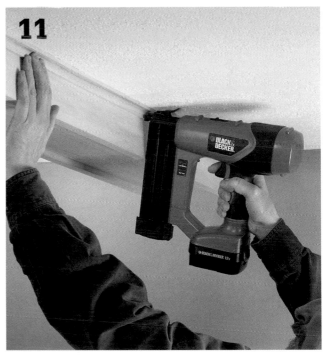

Install cove molding along the seam between the beams and the ceiling with 1¼" finish nails. Drive the nails into the sides of the beams. Apply the finish of your choice to the beams, filling the nail holes appropriately.

Hidden Rooms

Hidden rooms are not just for horror movies anymore. While they still have the mystique of old, today's hidden rooms also have practical purposes: many contain safes and secure storage. Some even include reinforced "panic rooms" where homeowners can hide in case of a break-in or other emergencies.

Whether it's for security or for the pure romance of the thing, a hidden room makes a fascinating and unique addition to your home.

The bookcase door systems on these two pages are mounted flat on the library wall and look like ordinary bookcases. But when pulled open, the hinged cases reveal a door opening into a safe or hidden room. See Resources, page 236

A library can offer entry to a hidden room or even a series of rooms in the guise of a normal-looking bookcase.

Wine Cellar Projects

A wine cellar provides a temperature—and humidity—controlled environment for storing a wine collection. For some people, that's all it needs to provide. For others, a wine cellar is more than a wine storage facility, it's a lifestyle choice. For these folks, the romance of a wine cellar is at least as important as its function.

When you have an appealing and well-stocked wine cellar, you're always ready to entertain friends and family. Add a wheel of Brie, some crackers, and a tray of crudités, and you've got a party—as well as a lovely place to hold it. For collectors, a wine cellar can be the centerpiece of their hobby. Racks, a computer, and tracking software all play a part in the lives of serious collectors.

This chapter gives you the fundamentals: light, temperature and humidity control, and then branches out to show you how to build wine racks and even a tasting table. By the end of the chapter, you'll be ready to build, outfit, and furnish a wine cellar where strolling violinists and accordion players would be right at home.

In This Chapter:

- Gallery of Wine Cellars
- All About Wine Cellars
- Installing Modular Wine Racks
- Building a Countertop Wine Rack
- Building a Tasting Table
- Installing Ceramic Tile on Concrete

Gallery of Wine Cellars

A glass-paneled exterior door opens into the controlled environment of this charming wine cellar. Stacked cases make excellent wine racks when securely attached to the wall.

Adding a serving surface to a wine rack creates an attractive tasting table without eating up additional space.

Custom wine racks are built to fit the dimensions of a cellar and to accommodate the preferences of the collector.

Custom features, such as a picture arch, inset cabinets, and built-in display cabinets, make this traditional cellar special. Custom crown and base moldings ease the transitions between the racks and the ceiling and floor.

Every element—from the lighted bar front and unique barstools to the oversized floor tiles—of this wine cellar has been chosen to complement the contemporary atmosphere.

A cantilevered ledge attached to an alcove in a stone wall makes a unique serving surface in this wine cellar.

Stone or tile floors are well suited to the cool environment of a wine cellar (plus, they're easy to clean).

All About Wine Cellars

When stored in a dark, cool, well-ventilated area where the temperature and relative humidity are fairly constant, wine improves with age.

For the serious vinophile, a successful wine cellar must be a controlled environment. The temperature, humidity, and light levels need to be kept within narrow ranges to safeguard a wine collection. After the environment is established, the issues of storage, such as racking, management, and appreciation of the collection, must be addressed. But if you also hope to use your wine cellar as a living space for tasting and casual dining, all of this controlling of the environment must be balanced with the requirements for creating a comfortable home.

Structural Fundamentals

You can build a wine cellar anywhere in your home, but it makes most sense in a basement where temperature, humidity, and light levels are easier to control. Starting with the right structure simplifies the process of establishing and maintaining the necessary temperature and humidity. Choose a location for your wine cellar that meets or can be modified to meet the following requirements.

- Walls and ceiling: Because the environment inside the wine cellar is deliberately manipulated to meet certain specific requirements, you'll want to make sure the room is well insulated. This not only allows you to control temperature and humidity more precisely, it helps you do it more efficiently. The walls should be insulated to a minimum of R-19, and the ceiling should be insulated to a minimum of R-30. All of the walls and the ceiling should have a 6 mil polyethylene vapor barrier on the warm side of the insulation: if the wine cellar is cooler than the surrounding area of the house, the vapor barrier should go between the insulation and the rest of the house; if the wine cellar is bordered by an exterior wall in a cold climate, the vapor barrier should go between the insulation and the interior wallcovering. Standard drywall is acceptable, but moisture-resistant greenboard is strongly preferred.

Typical wood wine racks are constructed from moisture-resistant wood, such as redwood, western red cedar, or mahogany.

- Flooring: Moisture-resistant surfaces, such as stone, tile, or brick, are ideal. Stone and tile floors should have a high friction coefficient so they don't become treacherous if moisture accumulates on them. Hardwood or cork are also appropriate.
- Door: An exterior-grade door with weatherstripping and a plate seal keeps the conditioned air inside the wine cellar. Glass doors should, at a minimum, be double paned.

Insulate walls and ceilings of your new wine cellar to help you control the temperature and humidity and save energy.

Temperature

For a collector of wine, the most important aspect of a wine cellar is the temperature, which should be kept as constant as possible and between 50 and 55°F. Any fluctuations should be very gradual because when exposed to temperature swings, the cork material and the bottle expand and contract, which can damage the cork seal and let oxygen into the bottle.

Wine stored at higher temperatures ages faster than wine stored at lower temperatures. Wine develops complexity as it ages, which means that slower is better. The temperature in your cellar should not drop below 50°F, however, or the wine may develop deposits and other suspensions. If you plan to use the cellar as living space, you will probably need to make some concessions on the relatively cool ideal temperature so the room can be enjoyed comfortably.

In large wine cellars, a cooling unit typically is employed to maintain optimum temperatures in your wine cellar. Most bear a resemblance to a room air conditioner, but in addition to cooling they also regulate humidity levels. If cooling the entire room isn't practical, consider buying a wine refrigerator. Wine refrigerators are available in sizes designed to hold everything from six to several hundred bottles. Some are quite attractive, too.

Wine should be stored at a temperature of 50 to 55°F and a humidity level ideally around 70%.

Relative Humidity

The relative humidity in a wine cellar should stay between 50 and 80 percent, with the ideal level being 70 percent. At lower humidity levels, corks can shrink and let air into the bottles. Higher levels of humidity won't necessarily harm the wine, but they do encourage the growth of mold and mildew in the room.

Light

Light, especially sunlight, can damage wine and cause it to develop unpleasant odors. Low levels of light are best, and incandescent or sodium vapor lights are better than fluorescent. Sparkling wines and wines in clear bottles are quite sensitive to light; wines in dark bottles are less susceptible.

Consider controlling the cellar's lights with motion-activated switches. The lights will come on the moment you step into the room and turn off moments after you leave.

If your cellar has windows, block their light as completely as possible. White roller shades block 80 percent of the light and heat gain from windows, so they make good first layers for window coverings. Top the roller shades with blackout draperies or louvered wood shutters, and you've got a winning combination.

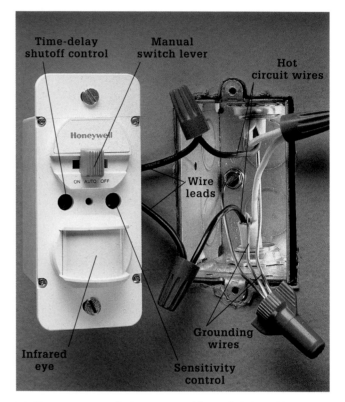

Motion-sensor switches use a wide-angle infrared beam to detect movement over a large area, which causes the lights to switch on. This is a good feature in dark rooms that are infrequently occupied. If the sensor does not detect movement for a period of time (usually around 15 minutes), the lights are shut off.

Decanting Wine ▸

Some older wines develop a considerable amount of sediment. Decanting them properly results in a more enjoyable drinking experience, and it's quite easy to do.

A day or two before you plan to drink the wine, stand the bottle upright so the sediment can settle to the bottom. When you're ready to decant the wine, slit the capsule and remove the entire seal from the neck of the bottle. Position a candle or small flashlight behind the neck of the bottle, and slowly, steadily pour the wine from the bottle into a clean carafe or decanter. Stop pouring when you see the leading edge of the sediment moving into the neck of the bottle. Save the half-glass or so of sediment remaining in the bottle for cooking purposes.

Ventilation

A well-ventilated wine cellar is a pleasant place to spend time, for you and for your wine. Odors develop in poorly ventilated space, and those odors may be absorbed by corks and even infiltrate the bottles. You can improve ventilation and air circulation by installing an exhaust fan, as in the cigar lounge project (page 88).

Poor ventilation can destroy wine over time. Adding an exhaust fan safeguards your collection and makes the cellar a more pleasant place. Exhaust fans are available in stylish light/fan combination products (as shown here).

Vibration

Vibration disturbs the sediment in wine, which can harm it over time. However, unless your home is next to a race track or a rail yard, it's unlikely that vibration will be an ongoing problem. It certainly makes sense to secure your wine racks to the walls or floor to protect them during earthquakes or other disasters, but if the worst happens, it's unlikely that the disruption of sediment will be the biggest problem you face.

Remember, though, that sounds are vibrations, too. The wine cellar should be located as far as possible from, for example, a home theater equipped with surround sound or the practice room for your garage band. If these spaces have to be within close proximity, soundproof them carefully.

Cleaning and Storing Wine Glasses ▸

You may be surprised to learn that your wine drinking experience can be impacted by how your wine glasses are stored and washed.

Sturdy glasses can be washed in the dishwasher if you use less detergent than usual and let them air dry rather than using the heat cycle. Delicate crystal requires more care. Washing soda (available in the detergent aisles of most grocery stores) absorbs residual odors or leftover wine and gently cleans the glasses. Rinse them thoroughly before drying.

Crystal can absorb odors from its surroundings, so be sure to store it well away from items that have strong smells, such as cleaning products, coffee, and so forth.

Storage

If you're starting a wine collection, learn about the proper angle of storage for different types of wine. Most wines are stored horizontally so the wine keeps the cork moist. Some collectors insist that the wine bottles should be stored with a slight slope toward the neck of the bottle to ensure that the cork is fully exposed to liquid at all times, but there appears to be little evidence that this makes any difference. Fortified wines, other than port, are stored standing. Talk with a wine dealer or a fellow wine lover about this important consideration.

In racks, storing the bottles with the labels up makes it easier to find the wine you want and allows you to see the sediment that collects on the bottom of the bottle.

Serving Temperatures ▸

- Serve sparkling wines well chilled, at 40 to 50°F, and serve white wines between 45 and 55°F.
- Serve full-bodied reds at 60 to 65°F and lighter, fruitier reds at 55 to 60°F.
- To chill a bottle of wine, put it in the refrigerator for an hour, the freezer for 30 minutes, or a bucket filled with ice and water for 15 minutes.

Insurance

If you have made a substantial investment in your wine collection, insure it. Smaller collections can be covered under your homeowner's policy as long as you have contents coverage that includes your wines. Larger collections should be covered by a stand-alone "valuable articles" policy that "blankets" the collection at a set value. Extensive collections should be insured on a bottle-by-bottle basis. Policies of this type cost around $.50 for every $100 worth of wine and depend on maintaining an accurate inventory.

Managing a Collection

Whether you're maintaining an inventory for your own entertainment or for investment purposes, cataloging your collection is an important step. Many software programs are available to help you track the "drink by" dates as well as the maturation dates and the values of your collection. Investigate several programs to compare features and costs before selecting one.

Kegerators ▸

If you are a beer lover too, you may want to add a kegerator (a refrigerator designed to cool and dispense a keg of beer) to your wine cellar. A kegerator keeps a tapped keg of beer fresh and fully charged for six to eight weeks or more. Kegerators are designed to be for indoor use only, and they need to be installed in locations with plenty of air circulation and grounded electrical receptacles. They should not be placed near heat sources or in direct sunlight.

The tap on a kegerator works in conjunction with a CO2 cartridge, and if the cartridge dries up, so does the kegerator's ability to dispense beer. Having a backup pump can save a party. A backup tap pushes air into the keg to dispense the beer. Make sure the pump you select works with the keg coupler on your kegerator. The pump and coupler have to lock together in order to work properly.

Refrigerated wine coolers help wines develop their fullest potential. Some models even have separate zones so each type of wine can be stored at its optimum temperature.

Installing Modular Wine Racks

Wine racks are the backbone of any wine cellar. If you are a skilled carpenter or woodworker, making your own wine racks is a fun exercise in designing and building. But if your ambition outpaces your experience, look into purchasing and installing a modular wine rack system. Sold over the Internet and at design centers, these systems allow you to design and install custom wine racks that fit your space, but at a fraction of the cost of hiring a professional carpenter to do the job. Most wine rack Websites have planning software so you can create the exact design you want.

Starting with the dimensions of your cellar, including ceiling height, you can design a racking system with just the right bottle capacity and bonus features for you. The assembly of most kits of this type requires only few tools and little or no expertise. If you can read and follow instructions, you can build a modular wine rack. The model shown here (see Resources, page 236) relies on a system of ladders and latches for assembly.

Wine racks should be secured to the walls in the cellar, especially if you live in an earthquake-prone area. Attach the rack to wall studs or use appropriate hardware, such as hollow wall anchors or molly bolts, designed for the approximate weight of the loaded racks.

Tools & Materials ▸

Hammer	Electronic stud finder
Drill	Wine rack kit
Carpenter's level	1¼" brads
18-gauge brad gun	2½" wood screws

A modular wine rack presents a host of design and configuration options.

How to Install a Modular Wine Rack

Design your wine rack system and order the components. Typical components you can choose from include full-height racks with a separate cubby for each bottle; box or diamond-shaped racks; curved racks, quarter-round racks, corner racks, racks with tasting shelves, and more. Open the containers and inspect the parts when the kit arrives. Make sure there is no damage and that nothing is missing.

The package will include complete assembly instructions. Base your assembly on these. To build the arrangement shown here, we started with the full-height rack, identifying the ladder-shaped standards and orienting them with the bottom ends aligned. The standards should be set parallel on a flat surface.

Attach spacer bars to the backs of the ladders at the prescribed rung locations, using finish nails or air-driven brad nails.

Wood Selection Tips ▶

Modular wine rack kits typically are sold in three or four wood species: cedar, redwood, red oak, and mahogany. The species you select will have a small effect on pricing, but the decision is primarily an aesthetic one. Western Red Cedar does not have an aromatic cedar scent, but is a clear, open-pored wood that produces a beautiful, mellow wood tone and does not require topcoating. Redwood is similar to cedar, but a bit denser and lighter in tone and with more limited availability. Red oak is harder and heavier and in most cases is stained and topcoated. Mahogany varies quite a bit, based on the country of origin (Malaysia and the Philippines, for example). It is a classic, open-pore wood with straight grain and good resistance to rot.

(continued)

4

5

Lift the ladders and spacer bar assembly so it is upright. Insert intermediate ladders between the end ladders you have connected with the spacer bars, following the manufacturer's recommended spacing. Attach the intermediate ladders to the front spacer bars (as shown), according to the manufacturer's instructions.

Continue to build the structure by adding the next ladder, repeating steps 3 and 4.

6

Finish attaching the final front spacer bars, and then move the unit into the desired place against the wall. Attach the assembly to the wall using 2½" screws driven through the back spacer bars. Make sure the assembly is level first, and drive the screws at wall stud locations (or use masonry anchors if walls are made of concrete or block).

Tip ▸

One of the great advantages of modular units is their ability to expand along with your collection. Through careful planning, you can create an elaborate storage system without breaking the bank. One approach is to start by designing your dream system and then dividing it into reasonable mini-projects.

7

Assemble the next modular unit according to the installation instructions. Position it next to the first unit, level it, and attach it to the wall. Some systems may suggest that you attach it to the first unit as well or that you install a trim piece to conceal the joint where they are connected. Continue installing modular units in the selected order.

8

Attach the last modular unit according to the installation instructions. Also install any trim pieces to conceal gaps between units and between the end unit and the wall. Most wood modular rack systems are either prefinished or designed to remain unfinished. Begin loading your wine collection into the racks.

Building a Countertop Wine Rack

Large wine racks have their places; so do smaller ones. You may want to showcase certain bottles or simply have them close at hand during a party or wine tasting. The rack shown in this project holds eight bottles and would make a nice gift for a new collector or even a noncollector who just likes to have a few bottles of wine at the ready.

We used clear birch for the rack, but any finish-grade, surface-planed hardwood will work just as well. And although we used a finish with a stain, you may choose to stain the wood first or even paint the rack. This is a matter of pure preference.

When building this rack, use regular carpenter's glue rather than the high-strength type. The regular type has a longer open time, which you'll probably need to get the entire rack assembled. If glue oozes out around the holes, wipe it off with a damp paper towel right away.

A countertop wine rack is an excellent way to showcase special bottles or to keep favorites within easy reach.

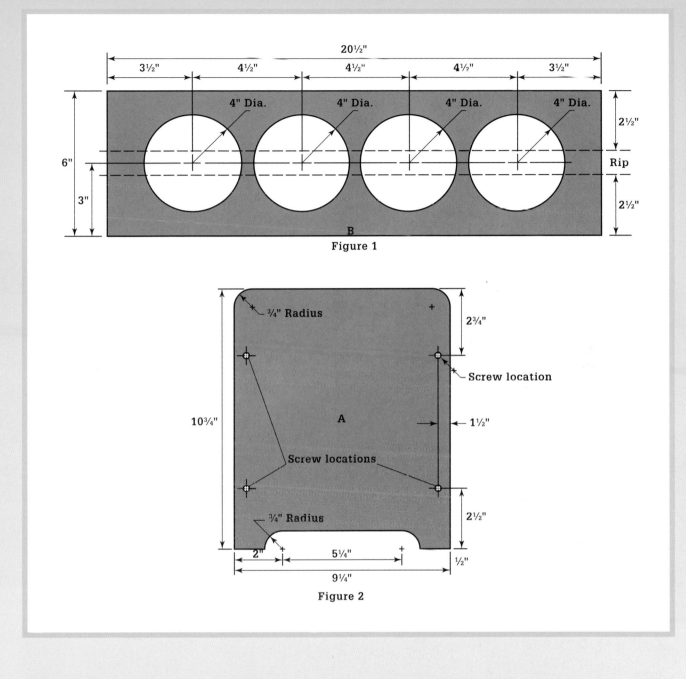

Figure 1

Figure 2

Tools

Circular saw
Jigsaw or coping saw
Drill
Rubber mallet
(3) Bar clamps

Materials

Transfer paper
#8 × 1¼" wood screws
Wood glue
Medium- and fine-grit sanding sponge

Polyurethane finish
Paintbrush
2 lineal ft. hardwood 1 × 10
4 lineal ft. hardwood 1 × 6

Cutting List

Key	Part	Dimension	Pcs.	Material
A	Sides	¾ × 9¼ × 10¾"	2	Hardwood
B	Shelf front/back	¾ × 6 × 20½"	2	Hardwood

How to Build a Countertop Wine Rack

1

Prepare stock as necessary for milling (we are using premilled 1 × 10 and 1 × 6 birch here—actual size is ¾" thick and 9¼" wide and 5½" wide). Cut the 1 × 10 board into two pieces, each 10¾" long. Cut the 1 × 6 into two pieces, each 20½" long.

2

Using a photocopier, enlarge the patterns on page 155. Transfer the rack pattern onto your 1 × 6 wood stock, using transfer paper and a stylus or hard pencil. Drill a ¼" hole near the edge of each circle, then slip the jigsaw blade into the hole and cut along marked lines to cut out the circles.

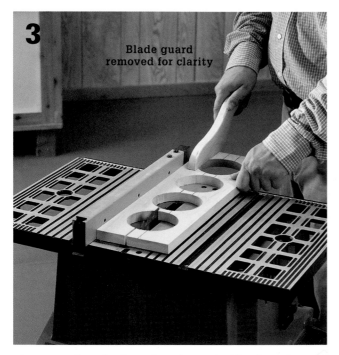

3

Blade guard removed for clarity

Rip-cut each rack piece along the marked line from the pattern, using a circular saw and straightedge guide or a table saw.

4

Transfer the side pattern onto each piece of 1 × 10. Mark the screw locations (see diagram on page 155), too. Cut along marked lines, using a jigsaw.

Use a router and a ¼" roundover bit to shape the edges of the panels (except the bottoms of the feet) and the edges of the racks (but not the ends). Sand the faces and edges of all the pieces.

Place end panels face-up on a workbench. Drill ⅜" countersunk pilot holes at marked screw locations. Spread glue on the ends of the rack pieces, assemble the pieces, and clamp the assembly together, using bar or pipe clamps.

Drive screws through the pilot holes in the panels and into the rack pieces. Spread glue on the ends of ⅜" dowel plugs or buttons and insert one into each screw hole to conceal the screw heads. Trim and sand the plugs flush after the glue dries.

When the glue is dry, sand the entire unit with a fine-grit sanding sponge and apply two coats of a finish of your choice.

Building a Tasting Table

Some wine cellars are strictly functional: that is, they are temperature- and humidity-controlled repositories for your cherished bottles of wine. But a wine cellar, especially a home wine cellar, can be much more than that. If you aren't thinking about including a table and perhaps seating in your wine cellar, you're missing an opportunity to create a room of high romance and appeal.

Tasting tables are one of the more popular members of the wine furniture family. Often, they are nothing more than an old barrel or cask set on end. All that is required is a small, sturdy surface where you can uncork a bottle and sample a glass or two. Some tasting tables have matching seating (usually bar stool height), while others are built with the presumption that busy wine tasters prefer a surface at a height that lends itself to imbibing while standing upright.

If you do a little searching around with wine furniture purveyors, you'll find that tasting tables often include wine racks in the table base. The tabletops are typically round in the French bistro fashion, and the prices range from a couple hundred dollars for flimsier models to a thousand or more for models with beefy hardwood butcher-block tops and very burly construction. The design you see here can be constructed with less than $30 worth of materials, but with a nice rich finish that will exhibit the Old World charm we've come to expect even in a contemporary wine cellar.

The tabletop is fashioned from ordinary SPF (spruce, pine, or fir) 2 × 4 stock that has been ripped down to 2½" wide to remove the bullnosed edges and give the table a slightly more streamlined appearance. The 2 × 4 stock is face glued to create a 24" × 24" square, from which the 24"-diameter round top is cut. Then, the top is banded with ⅛" strap iron. This is mostly for visual purposes, but the banding will help keep the top from warping as it expands and contracts.

If you'd prefer and you have a couple hundred dollars to spend, you can buy a preformed round butcher block. If you go this route, you might as well invest in the blocks that are a full 3" thick. And look for a maple or beech block that is formed with the end grain of the individual blocks pointing upward.

The table base is made from ordinary 1 × 4 pine and 21"-diameter MDF discs.

This lovely two-level tasting table adds a gracious touch to a wine cellar and provides a place to serve and enjoy a glass of your favorite vintage.

Tools

Table saw
Jigsaw
Compass
  or trammel points
Power sander
Drill
Hacksaw
Nut driver
Paintbrush

Materials

(20) black 1½"
  hex head
  lag screws
8d finish nails
  or 2" pneumatic
  nails
Wood glue
Shellac
Dark wood stain
⅛ × 1½ × 75½"
  strap iron
(4) 2 × 4" × 8 ft. SPF
(2) 1 × 4" × 8 ft. pine
(½ sheet) ¾" MDF
3" wood screws
2½" wood screws
Flat washers
1¼" brass wood screws

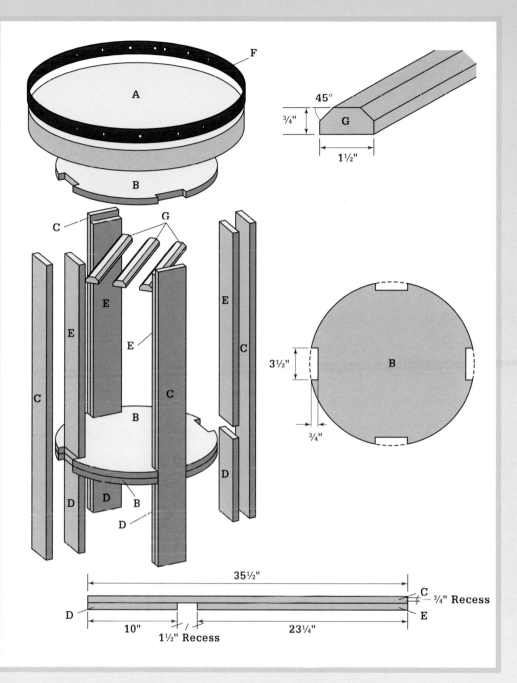

Cutting List

Key	Part	Dimension	Pcs.	Material
A	Tabletop	2½ × 24" dia.	1	1 × 4 Poplar
B	Shelf disc	¾ × 21" dia.	3	MDF
C	Leg	¾ × 3½ × 35½"	4	Pine
D	Filler-short	¾ × 3½ × 10"	4	Pine
E	Filler-long	¾ × 3½ × 23¼"	4	Pine
F	Metal strap	⅛ × 1½ × 75½"	1	Strap metal (cold rolled)
G	Stemware racks	¾ × 1½ × 12"	3	Oak (hardwood)

How to Build a Tasting Table

Select four 8 ft. 2 × 4s that are clear and straight, and then rip-cut them to 2½" wide by trimming ½" off each edge on a table saw to remove the bullnose profiles. Cut them to length (24") and lay the 16 workpieces face-to-face on a flat surface, forming a 24 × 24" square (A). Then, apply liberal amounts of wood glue to both surfaces and clamp the workpieces together firmly with several pipe or bar clamps. Let the glue-up cure overnight.

Use a compass or trammel points to lay out a 24"-dia. circle onto the tabletop glue-up. To make your own compass, tie a pencil to one end of a piece of twine, and then tie the other end of the twine to a nail so the nail and pencil point are exactly 12" apart when the twine is pulled taut. Drive the nail in the center of the glue-up. Then, pull the twine taut and trace a circular cutting line onto the glue-up.

Cut out the round shape using a bandsaw, if you have one, or a jigsaw with a wide, stiff wood-cutting blade. Cut just outside the cutting line so you can sand the edge up to the line on a stationary sander or with a belt sander.

Lightly resurface the tabletop with a belt sander and 150-grit sanding belt. This will get rid of dried glue squeeze-out and create a smoother, more even surface. Also finish-sand the edges.

5

Apply a coat of thinned shellac to the completely sanded tabletop as a sanding sealer. Let the sealer dry and then stain the tabletop with a dark wood stain, such as dark walnut. Once you have achieved the color tone you like, apply a penetrating topcoat if desired (such as wipe-on tung oil).

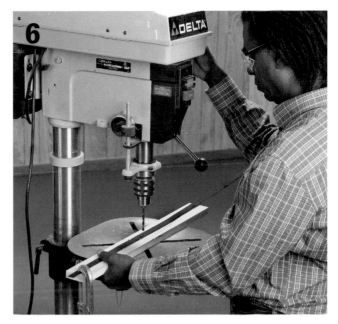

6

Purchase a piece of ⅛"-thick × 1½"-wide strap iron that's at least 76" long and cut it to length (75½", but measure the circumference of the top first to confirm). Also purchase square-head screws, preferably decorative black lag-style, and then drill a screw hole every 4" in the strap metal. Use a drill press when possible and lubricate the drilling area with cutting oil. Paint the strap with enamel paint.

7

Center the strap on the edge of the tabletop and mark a pilot hole for the first screw. Start in the middle of the strap (end to end). Drive a hex-head screw to fasten the strap. Then, add the next screw in line, and then the next on the opposite side. Alternate back and forth, bending the strap as you go so it is flush against the wood.

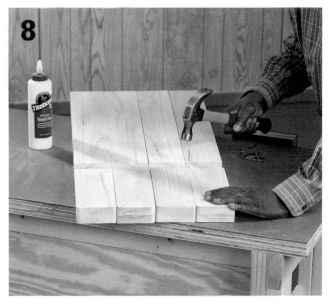

8

Cut the 1 × 4 stock for the legs, according to the cutting list. The legs are made by face-gluing the fillers (D, E) onto the inside faces of the full-length legs (C), creating a ¾" recess at the top and a 1½" recess starting 10" up from the bottom. Lay out the legs in a row so you know they're even, and attach the filler strips with glue and finish nails or pneumatic nails.

(continued)

Cut three 21"-dia. round shelves (B) from ¾"-thick MDF (medium-density fiberboard). Use the same compass technique shown in step 2 and the cutting technique shown in step 3. Once all three circles are cut, gang them together and sand them so the edges are round, smooth, and uniform.

Keeping the three circles ganged together, bisect the top circle to create four equal quadrants. Mark a centerpoint on the end of a short piece of 1 × 4 scrap. Then, position the scrap so the centerpoint aligns with each quadrant line and the back face of the scrap is flush with the edge of the disc assembly. Trace the scrap piece to create four notches for the 1 × 4 legs.

Cut out the notches with a jigsaw or bandsaw and sand them so they're smooth and square. Un-gang the three-circle assembly, and fill any nail or screw holes you may have created by ganging the parts.

Drill counterbored pilot holes for 3" wood screws through the leg notch areas and into the shelf discs. Attach the legs to the shelves with glue and screws. Test to make sure the base is level and square before filling the counterbores with wood plugs or wood filler.

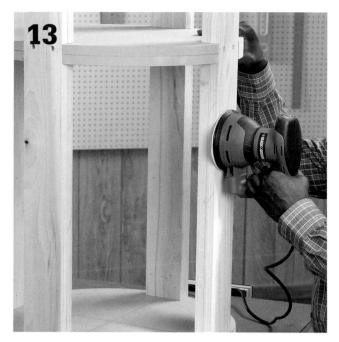

13

Finish-sand the legs and the circular shelves and apply the finish. Here, the same finish that's applied to the tabletop is applied to both the legs and the shelves (a sealer coat of thinned shellac followed by dark walnut stain and then penetrating oil). Because the stain is dark, the MDF shelves accept it well and blend with the legs and tabletop. But you may prefer to paint the shelves gloss black or even a metallic tone.

14

Set the tabletop good-side-down on a flat surface and then arrange the top of the base on the underside of the tabletop. The top should be centered, with an equal overhang (around 1½") all around. Drill several ¼"-dia. access holes through the top shelf in the base, but not into the tabletop. Then, drill pilot holes into the tabletop, centered on the access holes. Slip metal washers onto 2½" wood screws and drive one at each hole (using this washer and guide hole system allows for some wood movement).

15

Blade guard removed for clarity

Make a stemware rack to hang on the underside of the tabletop. Cut a 45° bevel that starts halfway up each edge of a strip of 1 × 2 hardwood. Cut the strip into three 12" lengths (G).

16

Arrange the three strips in parallel configuration on the underside of the top shelf. Use a wine glass as a reference for spacing the strips to create the rack. Keep the ends flush, and then attach the strips with counterbored 1¼" brass wood screws.

Installing Ceramic Tile on Concrete

Concrete, commonly found in basements, meets most of the criteria for a wine cellar floor—namely, moisture-resistant and nonslip. However, untreated concrete may not create the kind of romantic atmosphere you desire for your wine cellar.

Setting tile or flagstone on a concrete floor is a simple project. Its success depends on proper preparation of the concrete, a good layout, and attention to detail during the setting process. It's important to fill dips, cracks, and holes in the concrete with concrete patch or floor leveler before setting tile. If the surface is too uneven, the tile will crack when exposed to the pressure of foot traffic.

Choose tile or stone with enough texture to be a safe surface despite the moist conditions of your cellar. After you've chosen the tile or stone, ask your retailer about the appropriate mortar and grout for your application.

Before establishing reference lines for your project, think about where to start tiling. The goal is to continue working without having to step on previously laid tile. In many rooms it makes sense to start in the center, but since most wine cellars have only one door, it may be necessary to start at the far end of the room and move toward the door.

Tools & Materials ▸

Scrub brush	Concrete patching
4-ft. carpenter's level	compound
Square-edged trowel	Floor leveler
Paint roller	compound
¼" notched trowel	Concrete sealer
Tile saw	Ceramic or stone tile
Needlenose pliers	Thinset
Rubber grout float	or other mortar
Trisodium phosphate	Grout
Rubber gloves	

Stone or ceramic tile makes an ideal flooring for a wine cellar. It's durable, resistant to moisture, and easy to clean.

A wet saw is by far the best tool for homeowners to use to cut floor tile—especially extra-hard porcelain tile like we use here. They can be rented at reasonable daily rates. When possible, cut all tile at once (preferably outdoors) to economize on rental time. Before using the saw, read the manufacturer's directions and make sure you understand them. Wear safety glasses and hearing protection when using the saw and make sure the water container is full: Never use a tile saw without water.

Before You Start ▸

To be suitable for tiling, a concrete floor needs to be in good shape. If minor cracks and chips are patched with concrete patching compound before the tile is laid, they should not create any problems. But major cracks, crumbling concrete, and other concrete defects can cause the tile to fail as the problems telegraph through it. In some cases, installing an isolation membrane or membrane product is a sufficient preparation for tiling. Ask for information on this approach at your local tile shop.

How to Install Tile on Concrete

Scrub the floor with a solution of trisodium phosphate (TSP) and water, let it dry completely, and then check the clean concrete for cracks, holes, and other damage. Fill cracks and holes with concrete patching compound (see Before You Start, above). Apply concrete sealer to the clean, patched, and dry concrete. Use a paintbrush for the edges and the corners and a paint roller for the remaining areas.

Position a reference line (X) by measuring between opposite sides of the room and marking the center of each side. Snap a chalk line between these marks. Measure and mark the centerpoint of the chalk line. From this point, use a framing square to establish a second line perpendicular to the first. Snap a second reference line (Y) across the room.

(continued)

Test the layout by dry-setting one vertical and one horizontal row of tile, all the way to the walls in both directions. If the layout results in uneven or awkward cuts at the edges, adjust the reference lines to produce a better layout.

Mix a batch of thinset mortar, following the manufacturer's directions. Spread mortar evenly against both reference lines of one quadrant. Use a ¼"-notched square trowel to create furrows in the mortar bed.

Set the first tile in the corner of the quadrant where the reference lines intersect. When setting tiles that are 8" or larger, twist each tile slightly as you set it into position.

Using a soft rubber mallet, gently rap the central area of each tile a few times to set it evenly into the mortar. If the tile is not self-spacing, insert spacers at the corners of the tile.

7

Set tiles into the mortar along the reference lines. Cover a straight 2 × 4 with old carpeting and lay it across several tiles. Rap it with a mallet. Lay tile in the remaining area that has been covered with mortar. Work in small sections until you reach the walls. Cut tiles as needed (see page 165) using a wet saw.

OPTION: Irregular cuts can be made by scoring with a handheld tile cutter (top photo) and then finishing the cut with tile nippers (bottom photo).

8

Apply mortar directly to the backs of smaller cut tiles, instead of the floor, using the notched edge of the trowel to furrow the mortar. Set the tiles.

(continued)

9

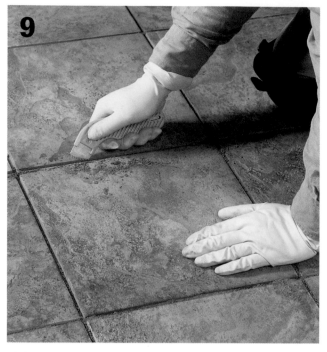

Finish installing the tiles. Inspect the joints between tiles and check for excess mortar. If necessary, use a utility knife to remove any high spots. If the mortar has dried, use a special tile tool called a grout knife to knock it down a bit.

Dealing with Thresholds ▸

Install threshold material (you can find these at any tile shop) in the doorway. Set the threshold in mortar so the top is even with the surface of the tile. Let the mortar cure for at least 24 hours.

10

Choose a sanded grout color that complements your tile. Mix a small batch of grout, following the manufacturer's directions. For unglazed or stone tile, add a release agent to keep the grout from bonding to the tile. *Tip: Dark grout doesn't show dirt but contrasts with lighter tile. Light grout is tough to keep looking clean. A midtone gray is often an excellent grout color.*

11

Starting in a corner, pour the grout over the tile. Spread the grout outward from the corner, pressing firmly on the grout float to completely fill the joints. Tilt the grout float at a 60° angle to the floor and use a figure-eight motion.

12

Use the grout float to remove excess grout from the surface of the tile. Wipe diagonally across the joints, holding the float in a nearly vertical position. Continue applying grout and wiping off excess until about 25 square feet of the floor has been grouted.

13

Remove excess grout by wiping a damp grout sponge diagonally over about 2 square feet of the tile at a time. Rinse the sponge in cool water between wipes. Wipe each area only once. Continue this process until you've grouted all the joints. Allow the grout to dry for about 4 hours, then use a soft cloth to buff the tile surface and remove any remaining grout film.

14

After the grout has cured completely (check manufacturer's instructions), apply grout sealer to the grout lines, using a small sponge brush. Don't brush sealer onto the tile surfaces, and wipe up any excess sealer immediately.

Home Spa Projects

Imagine this: It's the end of a long day. You wrap yourself in a thick terry robe and step through the door of your very own spa. As the door closes behind you, steam swirls, candles burn brightly, and essential oils linger in the air. The stress of the day melts away.

Luxury like this doesn't happen by accident. It takes careful planning and attention to detail: the electrical circuits, plumbing system, and the room's framing have to be ready to handle the additional loads placed on them by the transformation of an ordinary bathroom into a true spa.

The most luxurious home spa is one tailored to your personal interests and tastes. Evaluate the available space and create a plan that includes as many of your favorite amenities as realistically possible. Throughout this chapter, you'll find information and projects designed to help you create a luxurious home spa where you can treat yourself well every day.

In This Chapter:
- Gallery of Home Spas
- All About Home Spas
- Updating Wiring for Your Spa
- Glass Block Wall
- In-Floor Heating System
- Dual Showerhead
- Towel Warmer
- Air-Jet Tub
- Sauna

Gallery of Home Spas

Sunken tubs are romantic and exotic, but not always feasible given their structural requirements. Setting a deep tub into a raised platform creates much the same effect without the architectural challenges.

Pedicure thrones bring your feet within easy reach. Even if you don't have your own private esthetician, you and a friend or partner can take turns pampering and being pampered.

A tile tub deck creates an elegant sunken spa, and is much easier to install than its luxurious look would lead you to believe.

Wet rooms are tiled from floor to ceiling and sloped so water flows toward the drains. This example also includes a soaking tub shaped to cradle bathers in its depths.

Tower showers deliver water from every angle. Their adjustable jets can be set to produce invigorating bursts or relaxing sprays. They require a large-capacity water heater and a superior water-delivery system.

Here the whirlpool tub mounted in a tiled peninsula creates an elevated dais of personal comfort. Amazing luxury, but relatively simple to build.

Recessing a shower into a deep alcove can be an efficient use of space, especially if closets adjoin the alcove.

Nothing says luxury like ceramic tile. Don't confine it to floors and countertops—cover entire walls with it.

Large spaces invite large fixtures, such as this luxurious whirlpool set directly in front of a gleaming shower built to accommodate two.

Combination shower/baths are exceptionally popular, as they offer the best of both worlds in a space-saving arrangement.

In a whirlpool tub surrounded with river stone, a bather may feel as though they've taken a dip in a wandering stream.

All About Home Spas

A home spa is much like a bathroom, but usually larger and more luxurious. As such, they often include whirlpool tubs, power showers, and other amenities that place extra demands on your electric and plumbing systems, not to mention the floor framing. As you make plans to create a home spa, consider how they will impact each of the systems discussed in this section.

Electrical System

Whirlpool tubs, floor-warming systems, televisions and stereo systems, and even towel warmers require electricity. Some even require dedicated circuits. Before adding any appliance, evaluate the circuit you intend to use for the safe capacity. Also check the breaker box to make sure it can accommodate additional circuits.

Electricity and water can be a dangerous combination. Make sure all receptacles in your home spa are protected by a GFCI (ground-fault circuit interrupter). A GFCI is an important safety device that disconnects a circuit in the event of an overload, short circuit, or line-to-ground fault.

A GFCI constantly monitors electricity flowing in a circuit. If the current flowing through the circuit differs by a tiny amount from the current returning, the GFCI interrupts the power to the circuit within a fraction of a second.

Testing a GFCI ▸

- To test the receptacle GFCI, first plug a nightlight or lamp into the outlet. The light should be on. Press the "TEST" button on the GFCI. The GFCI's "RESET" button should pop out, and the light should go out.

- If the "RESET" button does not pop out, the GFCI is defective and should be replaced.
- If the GFCI is functioning properly and the lamp goes out, press the "RESET" button to restore power to the outlet.

All GFCIs should be tested once a month to make sure they are working properly and are protecting you from fatal shock. Also check the GFCI (before checking the circuit breaker panel) if you experience an unexplained loss of power.

Today's home spa can include amenities never before considered: a fireplace in the shower, video screens, and showers designed to recreate the feeling of bathing in a rain shower.

Plumbing System

Just as wiring systems may require upgrades to support new spa equipment, your plumbing system may need a boost if you want to install a high-volume shower or bath. Replacing your water heater with a larger capacity model is the most likely improvement, but there may be some cases where pumps, larger supply pipes, or other system additions are needed.

Whirlpool tubs hold between 50 and 150 gallons of water. Tower shower manufacturers recommend a hot water system capable of providing at least a first hour rating of 80 gallons. When making this type of upgrade, it may be necessary to purchase a large hot water heater or a tankless version. Tankless water heaters produce hot water on demand, so you never run out. The initial cost of these energy-efficient models may be offset over the long run, depending on your patterns of usage. Consult a plumber or plumbing supply retailer to discuss the best system for your home and spa.

Supply Pipe Sizing ▸

Water Supply Pipes: ¾" piping is required for many multihead showers. The standard in newer construction is ¾", but older homes may have ½" supply lines. In that case, supply pipes between the water heater and the shower need to be replaced.

Check Water Pressure ▸

Manufacturers of multihead and tower showers recommend a minimum running water pressure of 45 psi. Purchase a water-pressure gauge that screws directly onto an outdoor spigot or laundry supply faucet that's located near the spa room. Then turn on the water and read the psi (pounds per square inch) on the gauge. For inadequate water pressure, booster pumps are available.

Large-capacity jetted baths and high-consumption "tower showers" can consume hot water faster than a water heater may be able to heat it. A tankless water heater such as the one shown here may be the solution.

▌Walls and Floors

In remodeling projects, check the condition of the subflooring and make sure it can support added weight from the amenities you plan to add. The subfloor should be at least 1¼ inches thick. The easiest way to check the thickness of the subfloor is to pull out a cover on a heat register in the floor and look at its edges.

Whirlpool tubs and power showers are extremely heavy and often demand additional bracing in existing walls and floors. Research carefully and make sure you understand the requirements of the products you are purchasing. If you're not prepared to build in the additional support, hire a carpenter or contractor to do that part of the project for you.

Stone and tile make excellent wall and floor coverings in environments such as a spa, which tends to be humid. You might also want to use moisture-resistant, mold-resistant paint in areas that are painted.

Check the thickness and condition of existing subfloors before installing a new shower or any other heavy fixture. Removing a heat register grate may be all you need to do to evaluate the floor thickness.

Glass block is a superior choice for partition or shower walls in home spas. It's easy to work with and provides a reasonable amount of privacy without blocking precious light.

Updating Wiring for Your Spa

Every electrical circuit in a home has a "safe capacity." Safe capacity is the total amount of power the circuit wires can carry without tripping circuit breakers or blowing fuses. According to the National Electrical Code, the power used by light fixtures, lamps, tools, and appliances, called the "demand," must not exceed the safe capacity of the circuit.

Finding the safe capacity and the demand of a circuit is easy. Make these simple calculations to reduce the chances of tripped circuit breakers or blown fuses or to help plan the location of new appliances or plug-in lamps.

First, determine the amperage and voltage rating of the circuit. If you have an up-to-date circuit map, these ratings should be indicated on the map. If not, open the service panel door and read the amperage rating printed on the circuit breaker or on the rim of the fuse. The type of circuit breaker or fuse indicates the voltage of the circuit.

Use the amperage and voltage ratings to find the safe capacity of the circuit. Safe capacities of the most common household circuits are given in the table at right.

Safe capacities can be calculated by multiplying the amperage rating by voltage. The answer is the total capacity, expressed in watts, a unit of electrical measurement. To find the safe capacity, reduce the total capacity by 20 percent.

Next, compare the safe capacity of the circuit to the total power demand. To find the demand, add the wattage ratings for all light fixtures, lamps, and appliances on the circuit. For lights, use the wattage rating printed on the lightbulbs. Wattage ratings for appliances often are printed on the manufacturer's label. Approximate wattage ratings for many common household items are given in the table on the opposite page. If you are unsure about the wattage rating for a tool or appliance, use the highest number shown in the table to make calculations.

Compare the power demand to the safe capacity. The power demand should not exceed the safe capacity of the circuit. If it does, you must move lamps or appliances to another circuit. Or make sure that the power demand of the lamps and appliances turned on at the same time does not exceed the safe capacity of the circuit.

Safe Capacities for Circuits ▶

Amps × Volts	Total capacity	Safe capacity
15 A × 120 V =	1800 watts	1440 watts
20 A × 120 V =	2400 watts	1920 watts
25 A × 120 V =	3000 watts	2400 watts
30 A × 120 V =	3600 watts	2880 watts
20 A × 240 V =	4800 watts	3840 watts
30 A × 240 V =	7200 watts	5760 watts

How to Find Wattage & Amperage Ratings

Lightbulb wattage ratings are printed on the top of the bulb. If a light fixture has more than one bulb, remember to add the wattages of all the bulbs to find the total wattage of the fixture.

Appliance wattage ratings are often listed on the manufacturer's label. Or use the table of typical wattage ratings on the opposite page.

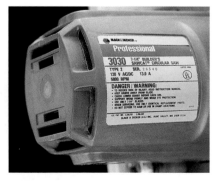

Amperage rating can be used to find the wattage of an appliance. Multiply the amperage by the voltage of the circuit. For example, a 13-amp, 120-volt circular saw is rated for 1560 watts.

Sample Circuit Evaluation

Circuit # __6__ Amps __20__ Volts __120__ Total capacity __2400__ (watts) Safe capacity __1920__ (watts)

Appliance or fixture	Notes	Wattage rating
REFRIGERATOR	CONSTANT USE	480
CEILING LIGHT	3 - 60 WATT BULBS	180
MICROWAVE OVEN		625
ELECTRIC CAN OPENER	OCCASIONAL USE	144
STEREO	PORTABLE BOOM BOX	300
CEILING LIGHT (HALLWAY)	2 60 WATT BULBS	120
Total demand:		1849 (watts)

Photocopy this sample circuit evaluation to keep a record of the power demand of each circuit. The words and numbers printed in blue will not reproduce on photocopies. In this sample kitchen circuit, the demand on the circuit is very close to the safe capacity. Adding another appliance, such as an electric frying pan, could overload the circuit and cause a fuse to blow or a circuit breaker to trip.

Typical Wattage Ratings (120-volt Circuit Except Where Noted) ▸

Appliance	Amps	Watts	Appliance	Amps	Watts
Air conditioner (central)	13 to 36 (240-v)	3120 to 8640	Garbage disposer	3.5 to 7.5	420 to 900
Air conditioner (window)	6 to 13	720 to 1560	Hair dryer	5 to 10	600 to 1200
Blender	2 to 4	240 to 480	Heater (portable)	7 to 12	840 to 1440
Broiler	12.5	1500	Microwave oven	4 to 10	480 to 1200
Can opener	1.2	144	Range (oven/stove)	5.5 to 10.8 (240-v)	1320 to 2600
Circular saw	10 to 12	1200 to 1440	Refrigerator	2 to 4	240 to 600
Clothes dryer	16.5 to 34 (240-v)	3960 to 8160	Router	8	960
Clothes iron	9	1080	Sander (portable)	2 to 5	240 to 600
Coffeemaker	4 to 8	480 to 960	Saw (table)	7 to 10	840 to 1200
Computer	4 to 7	480 to 840	Sewing machine	1	120
Dishwasher	8.5 to 12.5	1020 to 1500	Stereo	2.5 to 4	300 to 480
Drill (portable)	2 to 4	240 to 480	Television (color)	2.5	300
DVD player	2.5 to 4	300 to 480	Toaster	9	1080
Fan (ceiling)	3.5	420	Trash compactor	4 to 8	480 to 960
Fan (portable)	2	240	Vacuum cleaner	6 to 11	720 to 1320
Freezer	2 to 4	240 to 600	Waffle iron	7.5	900
Frying pan	9	1080	Washing machine	12.5	1500
Furnace, forced-air gas	6.5 to 13	780 to 1560	Water heater	15.8 to 21 (240-v)	3800 to 5040

Dimmer Switches

A dimmer switch makes it possible to set the lights in your spa to suit the moment—anything goes, from soft, romantic light to bright, task-oriented light.

Any standard single-pole switch can be replaced with a dimmer, as long as the switch box is of adequate size. Dimmer switches have larger bodies than standard switches. They also generate a small amount of heat that must dissipate. For these reasons, dimmers should not be installed in undersized electrical boxes or in boxes that are crowded with circuit wires. Always follow the manufacturer's specifications for installation.

In lighting configurations that use three-way switches, replace the standard switches with special three-way dimmers. If replacing both the switches with dimmers, buy a packaged pair of three-way dimmers designed to work together.

Dimmer switches are available in several styles. All types have wire leads instead of screw terminals, and they are connected to circuit wires using wire connectors. Some types have a green grounding lead that should be connected to the grounded metal box or to the bare copper grounding wires.

Tools & Materials ▸

Screwdriver
Circuit tester
Needlenose pliers

Wire connectors
Dimmer switch

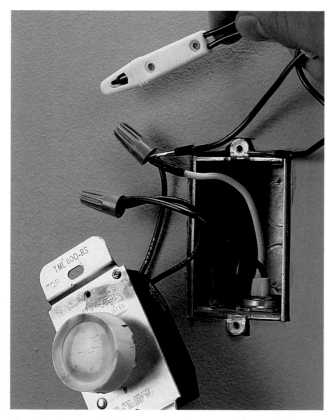

If replacing an old dimmer, test for power by touching one probe of the circuit tester to the grounded metal box or bare copper grounding wires and inserting the other probe into each wire connector. Tester should not glow. If it does, there is still power entering the box. Return to the service panel, and turn off the correct circuit.

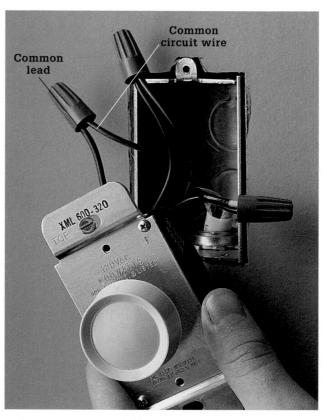

A three-way dimmer has an additional wire lead. This "common" lead is connected to the common circuit wire. When replacing a standard three-way switch with a dimmer, the common circuit wire is attached to the darkest screw terminal on the old switch.

How to Install a Dimmer Switch

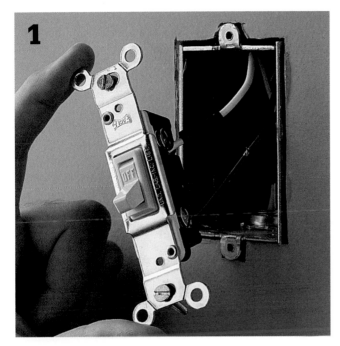

Turn off the power to the switch at the main service panel, then remove the coverplate and mounting screws. Holding the mounting straps carefully, pull the switch from the box. Be careful not to touch bare wires or screw terminals until they have been tested for power.

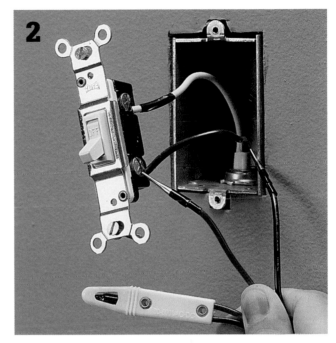

Test for power by touching one probe of the neon circuit tester to the grounded metal box or to the bare copper grounding wires and touching the other probe to each screw terminal. Tester should not glow. If it does, there is still power entering the box. Return to the service panel and turn off the correct circuit.

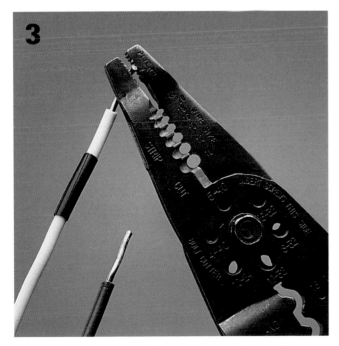

Disconnect the circuit wires and remove the switch. Straighten the circuit wires, and clip the ends, leaving about ½" of the bare wire end exposed.

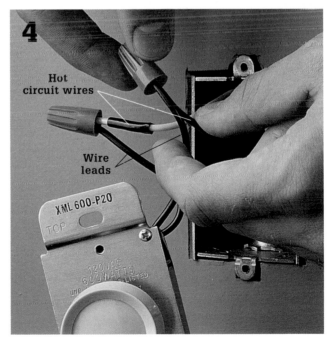

Connect the wire leads on the dimmer switch to the circuit wires, using wire connectors. The switch leads are interchangeable and can be attached to either of the two circuit wires.

Glass Block Wall

Glass block partition walls define space without cutting off light, which helps maintain a sense of openness in the room. Laying glass block doesn't require special tools or a lot of experience, and the block as well as the materials needed for the project are available at specialty distributors and home centers.

You can build your wall to any height. Top a low wall with a course of bullnose blocks to give it a finished rounded edge or with flat block to create a shelf. To build a full-height wall, calculate the number of courses of block you'll have, then frame-in a header to fill the remaining space between the finished block and the ceiling.

Follow these tips for a successful installation: When laying out your wall, keep in mind that glass block cannot be cut, so measure carefully. Lay-up the wall using plastic spacers set between the blocks. These ensure consistent mortar joints, and they support the weight of the block to prevent the mortar from squeezing out before it sets. Use premixed glass block mortar, available in dry-mix bags, in white and mortar-gray. When mixing the mortar, follow the manufacturer's directions carefully to achieve the ideal working consistency.

Because of its weight, a glass block wall requires a sturdy foundation. A 4-inch-thick concrete basement floor should be strong enough, but a wood floor may need to be reinforced. Contact the local building department for requirements in your area. Also bear in mind that glass block products and installation techniques vary by manufacturer—ask a glass block retailer or manufacturer for advice about the best products and methods for your project.

Tools & Materials ▸

Chalk line	16d common nails
Circular saw	Water-based
Jigsaw	asphalt emulsion
Paintbrush	Panel anchors
Drill	2½" drywall screws
Mixing box	Foam expansion strips
Trowel	Glass block mortar
Level	8" glass blocks
Pliers	¼" T-spacers
Jointing tool	Straight, flat board
Nylon- or	Reinforcement wire
natural-bristle brush	16-gauge wire
Sponge	Caulk or wall trim
2 × 6 lumber	Baseboard

Glass block is an exceptionally fine building material for spas. It transmits light but obscures views, a fine combination for bathing areas.

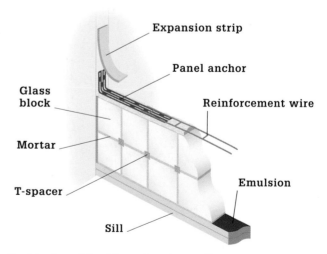

The block wall in this project has a sill made of two 2 × 6s cut to the exact width of the block. This provides a stable base to help resist floor movement and protect the lower courses. The block wall is secured to an anchor stud in an adjoining wall by means of metal panel anchors. Expansion strips between the two walls allow for movement.

How to Build a Glass Block Wall

Dry-lay the first course of glass block, using a ⅜" wood spacer between the wall and the first block, and ¼" spacers between the remaining blocks, to set the gaps for the mortar joints. Mark the wall position onto the floor, then remove the blocks. Snap chalk lines along the marks to create the sill outline.

Floor Reinforcement ▶

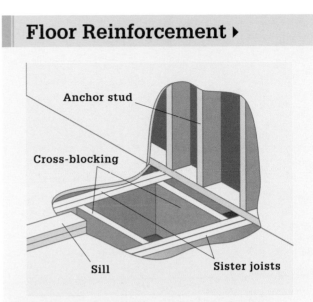

Anchor stud

Cross-blocking

Sill

Sister joists

If necessary, reinforce the floor joists nearest the new wall by installing sister joists and blocking that are the same size as the existing joists. If the new wall is not aligned with an existing wall stud, add an anchor stud centered at the new wall location. You can install the sill directly over the subfloor or over a suitable floor covering.

Determine the sill thickness based on the size of your baseboard and thickness of the floor covering. Rip 2 × 6 lumber to the width of the block. If the end blocks are shaped, trim the sill pieces to match, using a jigsaw. Fasten the sill to the subfloor and framing below with 16d common nails. Apply asphalt emulsion to the sill, using a paintbrush.

Mark plumb lines on the adjoining wall, straight up from the sides of the sill. Mark the finished height of each course along the lines. Fasten a panel anchor to the anchor stud at the top of every second course, using 2½" drywall screws. Cut expansion strips to size and adhere them to the wall between the anchors.

(continued)

Mix only as much mortar as you can apply in about 30 minutes. Lay a ⅜"-thick mortar bed on the sill, enough for three or four blocks. Set the first block, using ¼" T-spacers at the mortar joint locations (follow the manufacturer's directions for modifying T-spacers at the bottom and sides of the wall). Do not place mortar between blocks and expansion strips. Butter the trailing edge of each subsequent block with enough mortar to fill the sides of both blocks.

Lay the remainder of the course. If the wall has a corner, work from both ends toward the center, and install the corner piece last. Use ¼" T-spacers between blocks to maintain proper spacing. Plumb and level each block as you work, then check the entire course, using a flat board and a level. Tap blocks into place using a rubber mallet. Do not strike them with a metal tool.

At the top of the course, fill the joints with mortar, and then lay a ¼" bed of mortar for the second course. Lay the block for the second course, checking each block for level and plumb as you work.

Apply a ⅛" bed of mortar over the second course, then press the panel anchor into the mortar. Repeat this process at each anchor location.

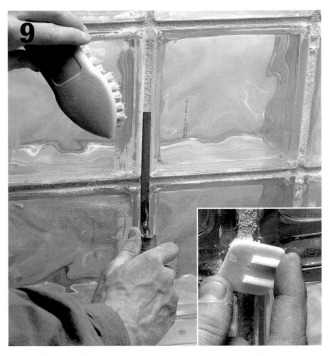

Add reinforcement wire in the same joints as the panel anchors, overlapping the anchors by 6". Also overlap the wire by 6" where multiple pieces are needed. At corners, cut the inner rail of the wire, bend the outer rail to follow the corner, then tie the inner rail ends together with 16-gauge wire. Add another ¼" mortar bed, then lay the next course of block.

Build the wall in complete courses, checking the mortar after each course. When it is hard enough to resist light finger pressure (usually within 30 minutes), twist off the T-spacer tabs (inset) and pack mortar in the voids. Then, tool all of the joints with a jointing tool. Remove excess mortar from the glass, using a brush or damp sponge.

Clean the glass block thoroughly, using a wet sponge and rinsing it often. Allow the surface to dry, then remove cloudy residue with a clean, dry cloth. After the mortar has cured for two weeks, apply a sealant. Caulk the seam between the glass block and the adjoining wall, or cover the gap with trim.

Reinstall the flooring, if necessary, then cut baseboard to fit around the sill. If the end of your wall has curved (bullnose) block, wrap the end with three pieces of trim.

In-Floor Heating System

Floor-warming systems require very little energy to run and are designed to heat ceramic tile floors only; they generally are not used as sole heat sources for rooms.

A typical floor-warming system consists of one or more thin mats containing electric resistance wires that heat up when energized, like an electric blanket. The mats are installed beneath the tile and are hardwired to a 120-volt GFCI circuit. A thermostat controls the temperature, and a timer turns the system off automatically.

The system shown in this project includes two plastic mesh mats, each with its own power lead that is wired directly to the thermostat. The mats are laid over a concrete floor and then covered with thinset adhesive and ceramic tile. If you have a wood subfloor, install cementboard before laying the mats.

A crucial part of installing this system is to use a multimeter to perform several resistance checks to make sure the heating wires have not been damaged during shipping or installation.

Electrical service required for a floor-warming system is based on size. A smaller system may connect to an existing GFCI circuit, but a larger one will need a dedicated circuit; follow the manufacturer's requirements.

To order a floor-warming system, contact the manufacturer or dealer. In most cases, you can send them plans and they'll custom-fit a system for your project area.

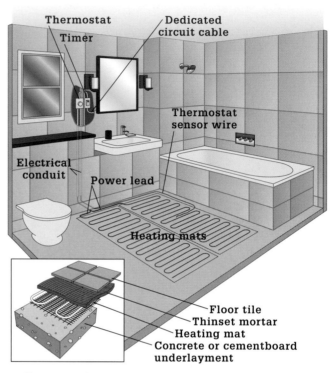

A floor-warming system requires a dedicated circuit to control its heating mats, thermostat, and timer.

Tools & Materials ▸

Multimeter	Single-gang
Drill	electrical box
Plumb bob	½"-dia.
Chisel	thin-wall conduit
Tubing cutter	Setscrew fittings
Vacuum	12/2 NM cable
Chalk line	Cable clamps
Grinder	Double-sided tape
Hot-glue gun	Electrical tape
Fish tape	Insulated cable clamps
Floor-warming system	Wire connectors
Tile	Metal connector plates
Thinset mortar	¼ × ⅜" square-
2½ × 4" double-gang	notched trowel
electrical box	Adapter cover

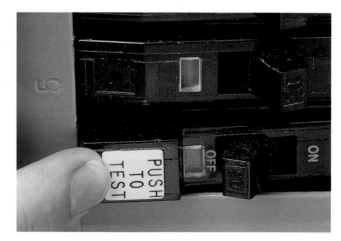

Floor-warming systems must be installed on a circuit with adequate amperage and a GFCI breaker. Smaller systems may tie into an existing circuit but larger ones need a dedicated circuit. Follow local building and electrical codes that apply to your project.

How to Install a Floor-warming System

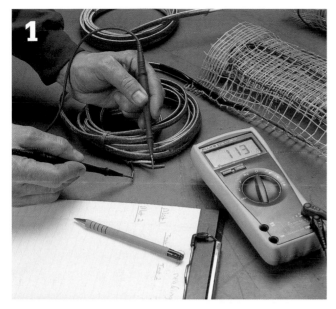

Check the resistance value (ohms) of each heating mat, using a digital multimeter. Record the reading. Compare your reading to the factory-tested reading noted by the manufacturer. Your reading must fall within the acceptable range determined by the manufacturer. If it does not, the mat has been damaged and should not be installed; contact the manufacturer for assistance.

Install boxes for the thermostat and timer at an accessible location. Remove the wall surface to expose the framing, then locate the boxes approximately 60" from the floor, making sure the power leads of the heating mats will reach the double-gang box. Mount a 2½"-deep × 4"-wide double-gang box (for the thermostat) to the stud closest to the determined location and a single-gang box (for the timer) on the other side of the stud.

Use a plumb bob to mark points on the bottom plate directly below the two knockouts on the thermostat box. At each mark, drill a ½" hole through the top of the plate, then drill two more holes as close as possible to the floor through the side of the plate, intersecting the top holes. (The holes will be used to route the power leads and thermostat sensor wire.) Clean up the holes with a chisel to ensure smooth routing.

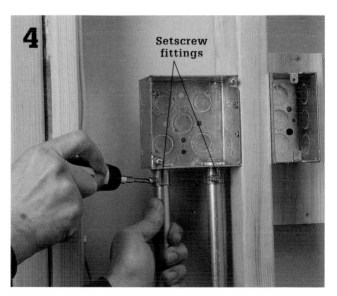

Cut two lengths of ½" thin-wall electrical conduit to fit between the thermostat box and the bottom plate. Place the bottom end of each length of conduit about ¼" into the holes in the bottom plate, and fasten the top end to the thermostat box, using a setscrew fitting. *Note: If you are installing three or more mats, use ¾" conduit instead of ½".*

(continued)

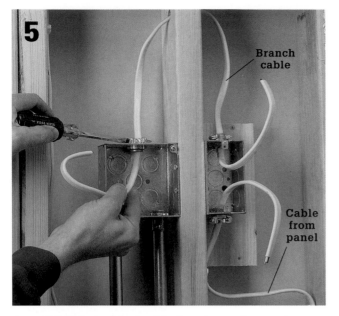

Run 12/2 NM electrical cable from the service panel to the timer box. Attach the cable to the box with a clamp. Drill a ⅝" hole through the center of the stud, about 12" above the boxes. Run a short branch cable from the timer box to the thermostat box, securing both ends with clamps. The branch cable should make a smooth curve where it passes through the stud. Protect the hole with a metal protector plate.

Vacuum the floor thoroughly. Plan the ceramic tile layout and snap reference lines for the tile installation. Spread the heating mats onto the floor with the power leads closest to the electrical boxes. Position the mats 3 to 6" away from walls, showers, bathtubs, and toilet flanges. You can lay the mats into the kick space of a vanity but not under the vanity cabinet or over expansion joints in the concrete slab. Set the edges of the mats close together, but do not overlap them: The heating wires in one mat must be at least 2" from the wires in the neighboring mat.

Confirm that the power leads still reach the thermostat box. Then, secure the mats to the floor, using strips of double-sided tape spaced every 24". Make sure the mats are lying flat with no wrinkles or ripples. Press down firmly to secure the mats to the tape.

Create recesses in the floor for the connections between the power leads and the heating-mat wires, using a grinder or a cold chisel and hammer. These insulated connections are too thick to lay under the tile and must be recessed to within ⅛" of the floor. Clean away any debris, and secure the connections in the recesses with a bead of hot glue.

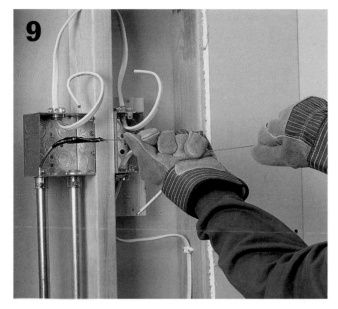

Thread a fish tape down one of the conduits, and attach the ends of the power leads to the fish tape, using electrical tape. Fish the leads up through the conduit. Secure the leads to the box with insulated cable clamps. Cut off the excess from the leads, leaving 8" extending from the clamps.

Feed the heat sensor wire down through the remaining conduit and weave it into the mesh of the nearest mat. Use dabs of hot glue to secure the sensor wire directly between two blue resistance wires, extending it 6" to 12" into the mat. Test the resistance of the heating mats with a multimeter (step 1, page 189) to make sure the resistance wires have not been damaged. Record the reading.

Install the ceramic floor tile. Use thinset mortar as an adhesive, and spread it carefully over the floor and mats with a ⅜" × ¼" square-notched trowel. Check the resistance of the mats periodically during the tile installation. If a mat becomes damaged, clean up any exposed mortar and contact the manufacturer. When the installation is complete, check the resistance of the mats once again and record the reading.

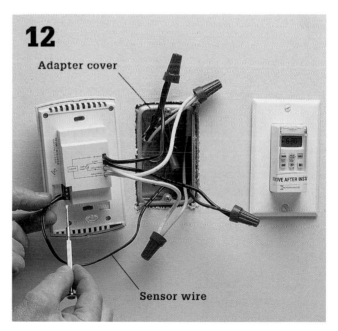

Adapter cover

Sensor wire

Install an adapter cover on the thermostat box, then patch the wall opening with drywall. Complete the wiring connections for the thermostat and timer, following the manufacturer's instructions. Attach the sensor wire to the thermostat setscrew connection. Apply the manufacturer's wiring labels to the thermostat box and service panel. Mount the thermostat and timer. Complete the circuit connection at the service panel. After the flooring materials have fully cured, test the system.

Dual Showerhead

What's more luxurious than a hot shower? Two hot showers at one time. That's what you get with a dual-head, multifunction shower such as the one shown in this project. Multiple showerheads let you aim the pulsing action at your neck and shoulders, your chest and legs, your hair and torso—you decide where you need it most.

Although some multifunction showerheads require elaborate and painstaking installation, others, such as the one shown here, take less than an hour, start to finish. This showerhead produces a lot of enjoyment in return for a reasonable investment of time and money.

At a flow of 2.5 gallons per minute, this showerhead won't overwhelm a water heater, either.

Unless you and your family members take longer showers to extend your enjoyment of its pleasures, it shouldn't radically increase your water usage or your utility bills.

Tools & Materials ▸

Pipe wrench
Dual-head
    multifunction
    showerhead
Fine-grit sandpaper
    or stiff bristle brush
Teflon tape
Soft rag or cloth
Electrical tape

Gentle streams, invigorating massage, soothing pulses—they're all available at the touch of a finger after you replace a standard showerhead with a two-head model.

How to Replace a Showerhead

Place electrical tape on the jaws of a pipe wrench to protect the metal showerhead parts from the teeth of the pipe wrench.

Grasp the end of the existing showerhead. Using a pipe wrench, turn the collar nut counterclockwise to remove the showerhead. Leave the shower arm and flange in place.

Carefully clean the threads at the end of the shower arm with fine-grit sandpaper or a stiff bristle metal brush. Be careful not to damage the threads. Run the water for a few seconds to flush debris from the arm.

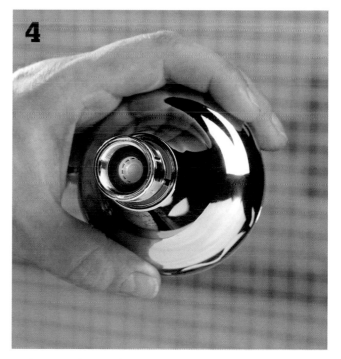

Make sure the pre-installed rubber washers are in place inside each showerhead as well as the shower arm's swivel nut.

(continued)

5

Wrap Teflon tape clockwise around the shower arm threads, making three or four loops of tape. Thread the shower arm extension from the new, dual-head showerhead onto the shower arm, turning clockwise. Hand-tighten firmly.

6

Wrap three or four loops of Teflon tape clockwise around the threads at each end of the shower arm extension.

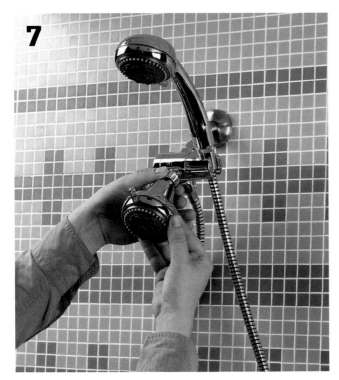

7

Install one showerhead on each end of the arm, hand-tightening them by turning clockwise. Wrap several courses of electrician's tape around the pipe wrench jaws and gently tighten the showerhead nut. Do not overtighten.

8

Adjust and rotate the showerheads as desired. Turn on the water and check for leaks. Gently tighten if necessary.

Tower Showers ▸

Showers have long been high on the list of people's favorite luxuries. What's not to love? The soothing warmth, the drumming of the water on your weary shoulders, the swirling steam—it's all comforting and comfortable. With today's innovations—multiple heads and steam generators—showers have moved into a whole new world.

There's little doubt that larger, more luxurious showers have become must-have items. A recent survey of architectural firms conducted by the American Institute of Architects reported a 63% increase in the number of requests for multiple-head showers in new construction and major remodeling projects.

Installation of a true tower shower, such as the model shown here, requires serious planning and a fair degree of technical expertise. These "Tower Showers" are also very expensive, easily reaching costs in the $5,000 range. Consult your plumbing retailer, a bathroom remodeling and design firm, or a licensed plumber to pursue this very high-end luxury.

Towel Warmer

Here's a little bit of luxury that need not be limited to high-end hotel stays. You can have heated towels in your own bathroom with an easy-to-install towel warmer. In a relatively cold room, this can make stepping out of the shower a much more pleasant experience.

Heated towel racks are available in a wide range of styles and sizes. Freestanding floor models as well as door and wall-mounted versions can be plugged in for use when desired. Hardwired wall-mounted versions can be switched on when you enter the bathroom so your towels are warm when you step out of the shower. Although they require some electrical skills, the hardwired models do not need to be located near wall receptacles, and they do not have exposed cords or extension cords hanging on the wall. However, if you locate the warmer directly above an existing receptacle, you can save a lot of time and mess by running cable up from the receptacle to the new electrical box for the warmer.

Before installing hardwired models, check your local electrical codes for applicable regulations. If you are not experienced with home wiring, have an electrician do this job for you or opt for a plug-in model.

Tools & Materials ▸

Drill
Level
Keyhole saw
Wiring tools
Phillips screwdriver
Stud finder

Retrofit electrical outlet box
Wire connectors
NM cable
Towel warmer
Masking tape
Cable clamp

A hard-wired towel warmer offers the luxury of heated towels without the safety concerns of a plug-in device.

How to Install a Hardwired Towel Warmer

Use a stud finder to locate the studs in the area you wish to place the towel warmer. Mark the stud locations with masking tape or pencil lines. Attach the wall brackets to the towel warmer and hold the unit against the wall at least 7" from the floor and 3" from the ceiling or any overhang. Mark the location of the wall bracket outlet plate, where the electrical connection will be made, and the mounting brackets.

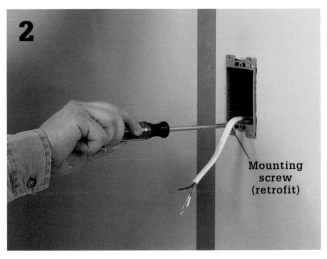

Mounting screw (retrofit)

Shut off electrical power at the main service panel. At the mark for the wall bracket outlet, cut a hole in the wallcovering for a retrofit electrical box. Run NM cable from the opening to a GFCI-protected circuit (here, we ran cable down to a receptacle directly beneath it), or install a separate GFCI-protected circuit (you'll need to consult a wiring book or an electrician). Pull the cable through the hole in the retrofit box, and then tighten the cable clamp. Place the box in the hole flush with the wall surface and tighten the mounting screw in the box. Cut the wires so about 5" extends into the box and strip the insulation off at ⅜" from the end of each wire.

Position the towel warmer over the outlet box and mark the locations of the screw holes for the wall brackets. Make sure the appliance is level. Remove the warmer and drill ¼" pilot holes at the marked locations. If the marks are located over studs, drill ⅛" pilot holes. If not, push wall anchors into the holes. Thread the mounting screws through the brackets. Have a helper hold the towel rack in place and use wire connectors to connect the wires, including the ground wire, according to the instructions.

Once the electrical connections are made, fasten the towel rack brackets to the wall. Turn on power and test the towel warmer. Finally, attach the electrical cover plate with an integral on/off switch.

Air-jet Tub

A jetted spa is basically a bathtub that recirculates water, air, or a combination of the two to create an effect known as hydromassage. Hydromassage increases blood flow, relieves pressure on joints and muscles, and relieves tension. Interior hydromassage tubs usually have a water pump that blows a mixture of air and water through jets located in the tub body. Many include an integral water heater.

The product you'll see installed on these pages is a bit different. It is an air-jet tub: a relatively new entry in the jetted spa market that circulates only warm air, not water. This technology makes it safe to use bath oils, bubble bath, and bath salts in the spa. A model with no heater requires only a single 120-volt dedicated circuit. Models with heaters normally require either multiple dedicated 120-volt circuits or a 240-volt circuit.

Like normal bathtubs, jetted tubs can be installed in a variety of ways. Here, we install a drop-in tub (no nailing flange) in a 3-wall alcove. This may require the construction of a new stub wall, like the short wall we plumbed as the wet wall for this installation.

Unless you have a lot of wiring and plumbing experience, consider hiring professionals for all or parts of the project.

Tools & Materials ▶

Plumbing tools	Shims
Utility knife	1 × 4 lumber
4-foot level	1½" galvanized
Square-edge trowel	deck screws
Drill or power driver	1" galvanized
Channel-type pliers	roofing nails
Hacksaw	Plumber's putty
Level	Dry-set mortar
Circular saw	Trowel
Drill	Silicone caulk
Screwdriver	Jetted tub
Adjustable wrench	Faucet
Drain-waste-	Plumbing supplies
overflow assembly	

Air-jet tubs create massaging action, stirring the water with warm air. Air-jets eliminate concerns about stagnant water and bacteria that can remain in the pipes of whirlpool tubs.

How to Install an Air-jet Tub

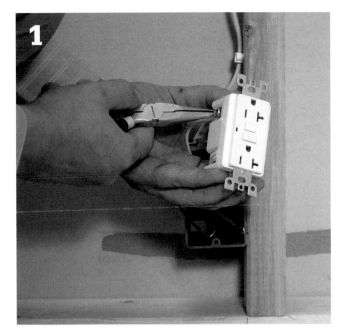

1

2

Prepare the site for the installation. Remove wall coverings in the installation area to expose bare studs. Provide a dedicated electrical circuit or circuits to the tub area according to the specifications in your installation manual (hire an electrician if you are not comfortable with wiring). This model plugs into a GFCI-protected receptacle on a dedicated 120-volt circuit.

Make framing improvements such as adding 1 × 4 bracing at supply risers and the faucet body location. For drop-in tubs that do not have nailing flanges, you may need to add short stub walls to provide a stable resting point. Here, a short stub wall was installed at one end to serve as the tub wet wall.

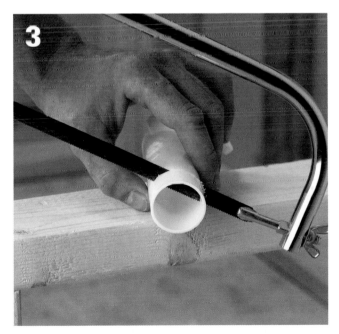

3

4

Floor leveler compound

Cut the drain tailpiece to length depending on the distance you'll need to span to the trap. Use a hacksaw or tubing cutter to make the cut.

Prepare the floor or subfloor. Check with a level and fill any dips with floor leveling compound or mortar. If there is a joint in the subfloor in the installation area, make sure the sides are level. (The floor has to be level in order to support the weight of the tub, the water, and bathers.) Also make sure there is no rot or disrepair in the structural elements.

(continued)

Test the tub fit. First, cut a piece of the shipping carton to fit inside the tub and protect its surface. Have someone help you slide the tub into the installation area, flush against the wall studs, so you can check the fit. *Tip: Lay a pair of 1 × 4s perpendicular to the tub opening and use them as skids to make it easier to slide the tub in. Remove the skids and lower the tub on the floor.*

Set a 4-ft. level across the rim of the tub and check it for level. If it is not level, place shims under the tub until it is.

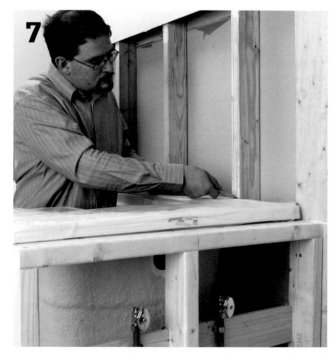

Mark the top of the tub's rim or nailing flange at each stud as a reference for installing additional supports or ledgers. Remove the tub from the alcove.

Add support frames or ledgers as directed by the manufacturer and secure them in the installation area so the top of the tub or nailing flange will be at the height you scribed in step 7.

9

Assemble the drain-waste-overflow kit to fit the drain and overflow openings, following the tub manufacturer's directions. Install the D-W-O kit (it is virtually impossible to attach it once the tub is in place).

10

Fasten the threaded parts of the drain assembly. A ring of plumber's putty between the drain coverplate and the tub will help create a good seal. If you will be installing a pop-up drain, install it now as well.

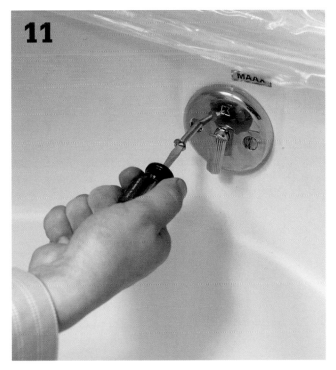

11

Attach the overflow coverplate so it conceals the overflow opening. Adjust the pop-up drain plug linkage as directed by the manufacturer.

12

Begin the actual installation. For some tubs, it is recommended that you trowel a layer of thinset mortar in the installation area. But read your instructions carefully. Many tubs feature integral feet that are meant to rest directly on the floor.

(continued)

13

Slide the tub back into the opening. Remove the skids, if you are using them. Press down evenly on the tub rims until they make solid contact with the ledgers or frames.

14

Provide support for the tub on the open side if it does not have a structural skirt. Here, a 2 × 4 stub wall is built to the exact height of the underside of the rim and then attached in place. Screw it to both end walls and to the floor.

Tip ▸

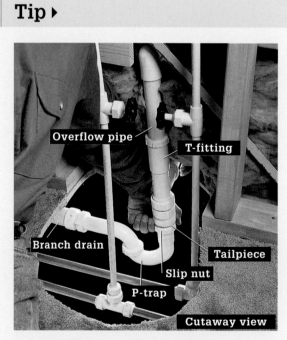

Overflow pipe

T-fitting

Branch drain

Tailpiece

Slip nut

P-trap

Cutaway view

Make the plumbing drain connections before you proceed further. To connect the drain tailpiece to the trap you will need access either from below or from an access panel. The photo above shows a typical tub drain configuration seen cutaway through the floor.

15

Cover the gaps in the wallcoverings around the tub. Here, cementboard is installed in preparation for a tile backsplash. If your tub has nailing flanges, attach strips of metal flashing to the wall so they extend down to within about ¼" of the tub rim. If your tub has a removable apron, install it.

16

Make wiring connections according to the tub manufacturer's instructions. The requirements vary greatly among jetted spas. Some municipalities may require that a licensed professional do this work. Here, the airflow regulator is being wired. Note that most codes have a safety requirement that the on/off switch must be located so it cannot be reached by a bather in the tub.

17

Test the operation of the jetted spa before you finish the walls or deck in case there is a hidden problem. Fill it with a hose if you have not installed the faucet (the faucet normally is installed after the wall surfaces, unless you are deck-mounting the faucet on the tub rim). Run the spa. If it works, go ahead and drain the water.

18

Finish the wall surfaces. Here, a tile surround and backsplash is being installed over the cementboard backer.

19

Hook up the faucet to the water supply plumbing according to the manufacturer's directions (or have your plumber do the job). Remove the aerator from the tip of the spout and run water through it to clear out any debris. Attach the aerator, fill the tub, and have yourself a nice, relaxing soak.

Sauna

A Scandanavian tradition for centuries, the sauna has become increasingly popular in North America. The traditional sauna cycle of intense heat followed by a cooling shower helps to soothe, relax, and invigorate the body while providing health benefits such as reduced muscle tension and clean, refreshed skin.

Saunas are typically lined with softwoods, such as cedar, redwood, pine, or spruce, all of which lend a comforting, organic feel to the space. Woods that stay comfortable to the touch at high heat, such as abachi, aspen, and hemlock, are often used for the benches and backrests.

Manufactured saunas generally are sold as either prefabricated or custom-cut kits. Both types include the pre-hung door, benches, electric heater unit, and other accessories. The prefab kits also include finished and insulated wall and ceiling panels, which allow for quick and easy installation.

Custom-cut sauna kits typically are less expensive than prefab kits, but more complicated, requiring you to frame and insulate the space prior to installation. You supply the manufacturer with your project dimensions and they deliver precut and labeled tongue-and-groove boards for the interior paneling. Consult with your manufacturer or dealer about your sauna plans before beginning the framing process.

As you plan the location of your sauna, keep in mind that the flooring should be a water-resistant surface such as concrete, resilient flooring, or ceramic tile. Locating the sauna near a floor drain will ease cleaning.

Check with your manufacturer before attempting to install and connect the electrical wiring for your sauna's systems. Some manufacturers' warranties require that all electrical work be completed by a licensed electrician.

When framing your sauna, use pressure-treated 2 × 4s for the bottom plates for added moisture protection. The rest of the framing can be built with standard 2 × 4s.

Custom-cut saunas can be tailored to any space or design. This unique hex-shaped sauna includes design elements such as shielded cove lighting, vertical paneling, and mounted backrests.

Tools & Materials ▸

Tape measure	2 × 4s
Chalk line	(for framing)
4-ft. level	Caulk
Circular saw	Galvanized
Caulk gun	common nails
Powder-actuated	(8d, 10d, 16d)
nailer	3½" unfaced
Hammer	fiberglass
Stud finder	insulation
Plumb bob	⅜" staples
Stapler	1½" galvanized
Pneumatic nailer	pin nails or
and compressor	4d galvanized
Drill	finish nails
Custom-cut	3" stainless steel
sauna kit	screws
Treated 2 × 4s	Exterior wall
(for bottom	material
plates)	Foil tape

How to Install a Custom-cut Sauna

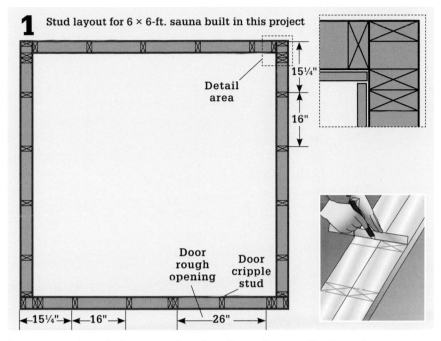

1 Stud layout for 6 × 6-ft. sauna built in this project

Detail area

15¼"

16"

Door rough opening

Door cripple stud

←15¼"→ ←16"→ ←—26"—→

Measure and mark the sauna framing dimensions on the floor, then snap chalk lines to mark your framing layout. Cut bottom plates from treated 2 × 4s, then mark the 16" on-center stud layout onto the plates. Include the door rough opening and extra nailer studs in the corners to allow for fastening the tongue-and-groove boards (detail). Cut top plates to length, pair them with bottom plates, and transfer the stud markings to the top plates (inset). Caulk beneath the bottom plates, then fasten them to the floor, using 16d nails (or use masonry screws or a powder-actuated nailer on a concrete floor).

2

The sauna door requires a double plate to provide a proper sill. Transfer the stud layout markings to another 2 × 4 and install it on top of the front wall plate, using 10d nails driven at a slight angle.

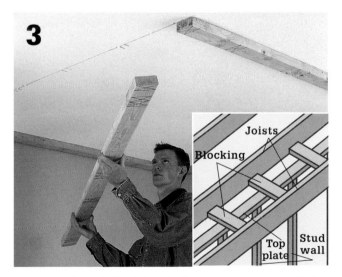

3

Joists

Blocking

Top plate

Stud wall

Locate and mark the joists in the area, using a stud finder. If a wall falls between parallel joists, remove the ceiling drywall and install 2× blocking between the joists (inset). Use a plumb bob to transfer the plate locations from the floor to the ceiling, then snap chalk lines through the ceiling marks. Attach the top plates to the joists or blocking, using 16d nails.

4

Measure and cut the wall studs to length from standard 2 × 4s. Install the studs by toenailing them through the sides of the studs and into the top and bottom plates, using 8d nails. On each end, drive two nails through one side of the stud and one more through the center on the other side.

(continued)

5

Install the king studs for the door frame. Make sure that these studs are plumb, using a level. Cut and install a 2 × 4 header flat between the king studs, using 16d nails. Cut and install jack studs to fit snugly beneath the header. Cut and install a cripple stud above the header, centered over the rough opening.

6

Measure up 7 ft. from the floor and mark a stud. Use a 4-ft. level to transfer the mark across the studs. Align 2 × 4 nailers on the marks and attach them to the studs with 16d nails. Mark the joist layout onto the nailers, using 16" on-center spacing. Cut 2 × 4 joists to fit and fasten them to the nailers, using 10d nails. *Note: If the joist span is over 8 ft., use 2 × 6s for the nailers and joists.*

7

Frame openings for the sauna vents according to the manufacturer's directions. Locate the framing for the inlet vent at floor level, near the heater. Frame the outlet vent on another wall, located just below the top bench height (about 30"). If you have a wall-mount heater unit, attach 2 × 4 supports between the studs at the heater location according to the manufacturer's directions.

8 Possible Electrical Configuration

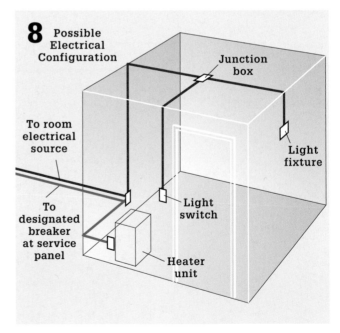

Install electrical boxes and route cable to the lights, switches, and heater unit as directed by the manufacturer. *Note: Some manufacturers or municipalities may require that all electrical work be completed by a licensed electrician.*

9

Install a double layer of 3½" unfaced fiberglass insulation at the ceiling. Lay the first layer on top of the ceiling framing, perpendicular to the joists. Install a second layer between the joists. If necessary, drive nails partially into the joists to hold the second layer in place.

10

Install insulation between the studs along the finished walls. For easier access while paneling the sauna, leave the outer walls open until you are ready to panel them. (See step 15.) Install the included vapor barrier over the insulation on the walls and ceiling, attaching it to the framing with ⅜" staples. Begin at the bottom of the walls and overlap the foil pieces as you go up. Repair tears and seal joints with foil tape.

11

Install the precut ceiling boards, starting at the back of the sauna. If the boards are slightly shorter than the framing, split the difference and allow equal space on each side. Nail the first board to the joists through its face, then "blind-nail" the board by driving 1½" galvanized pin nails (or 4d galvanized finish nails) at an angle through the inside of the tongue. If you are not using a pneumatic nailer, drive the nail heads below the wood surface with a nail set. For the remaining boards, fit the groove over the tongue of the preceding board and drive nails through the inside of the tongue only.

12

Measure periodically to make sure the boards are straight and parallel to the far wall, adjusting the remaining few boards, if necessary. When you get to the final board, measure the space remaining, rip the board to fit, and face-nail it into place.

(continued)

Check to see if the floor is level by moving a level across the floor. If it is uneven, mark the high point. Measure down from the sauna ceiling to this point and subtract ½". Use this measurement to mark the starting point for the tongue-and-groove wallboards at all four corners. This will allow for a minimum ½" gap between the boards and the floor.

Align the first board with the starting marks along the back wall and attach it to the studs, using the blind-nailing techniques shown in step 11. Trim the boards, as necessary, to fit around the vent openings. Check the boards for level every few rows, and adjust the next few rows slightly if the boards fall out of level.

Variation: If you are installing the paneling vertically, install 1 × 2 furring strips over the studs, spaced 24" on-center, using 8d nails. Install the boards, starting in the corner farthest from the heater. Finish the two walls going toward the heater, then complete the other two walls.

On the open stud walls, finish the exterior with the desired paneling or drywall. Then, install the insulation and vapor barrier, as shown in step 10. Finish installing the tongue-and-groove paneling on the interior side of the walls.

Measure from the floor and mark the side walls at 12" and 30" for the bench supports. Align the top edge of each support with the marks and fasten them to the wall studs with 3" screws. Install the prebuilt benches, attaching them to the supports with 3" screws.

17

Position the door in the framed opening with the jamb flush with the exterior wall surface. Check that the door is level, plumb, and centered, shimming, if necessary. Fasten the hinge side to the 2 × 4 frame with the included screws. Check the door again for level, then continue to fasten around the frame.

18

Setback

Door jamb extension

If necessary, install the door jamb extensions flush with the interior wall surface, fastening them to the door frames using 4d finish nails. Mark a setback to indicate the inside edge of the door casings on each of the jambs. Install the casings around the interior and exterior of the door, using 4d galvanized finish nails.

19

Install trim molding to cover the joints at the wall and ceiling corners, cutting the pieces as needed. Fasten the trim with 4d galvanized finish nails. Install the inlet and outlet grills over the vent openings, using the included screws.

20

Install the heater unit, control panel, and light fixtures according to the manufacturer's directions. Assemble and install the heater guard around the heater unit, positioning the top edge of the guard just below the exposed rocks. Follow the manufacturer's directions for operating the heater unit.

Outdoor Projects

Afternoons spent on a bench beside a fountain, reading a good book; working on your putting game alone or with friends; listening to the sounds of running water and watching the wildlife it attracts: These are just a few of the luxuries that await you when you undertake the projects in this chapter.

Outdoor projects for luxurious living do more than improve your yard; they offer opportunities to improve your life. With the right attitude and the right amenities, you can move the party outside where you can enjoy fresh air, sunshine, and playtime with family and friends. The interesting and easy projects found in these pages will provide hours of entertainment for you and your family. The actual building of the projects should be most enjoyable; using them could be even more fun.

In This Chapter:

- Gallery of Outdoor Living
- All About Outdoor Projects
- Installing a Backyard Putting Green
- Installing a Garden Pond & Fountain
- Creating a Free-form Meditation Pond

Gallery of Outdoor Living

A courtyard fountain treats you to cascading streams of water at each arrival and departure from home.

A floating fountain creates drama and freshens the water in ponds and pools. Lighted jets contribute interest to the landscape, day and night.

A stone frog adds a refreshing touch of whimsy to this garden pond. Jets of this type, sometimes called spitters, are easy to install and simple to maintain.

Colorful fish, such as these koi, bring life and energy to a garden pond. They're not for everyone, though. Make sure you have the time and patience necessary before introducing them to your pond.

The ultimate in low-maintenance, a stone landscape with pools of water offers the perfect place to meditate or to think deeply.

Sloped, curving layouts offer realistic situations and the opportunity to practice difficult shots. Design a green and plan pin placement that allows you to recreate shots that give you the most trouble.

Artificial putting greens can be assembled in your yard and removed and stored during the off-season.

Surprisingly easy to install, putting greens provide hours of fun for golf enthusiasts.

All About Outdoor Projects

In recent years we've collectively stretched the boundaries of what we consider "home" to include our yards and landscapes. Establishing "rooms" with walls and floors and activity spaces makes an outdoor home more inviting and accessible. Here are some things to consider when working on outdoor projects.

Gardening in water can be as rewarding as gardening in soil and can produce just as much beauty. It requires a bit of specialized knowledge and the willingness to roll up your sleeves and get wet once in a while.

Safety First

Many outdoor projects begin with excavation. Before you start construction on any project that involves digging, contact your utilities suppliers to have your utility lines flagged by one of their technicians. This isn't merely a suggestion; in most states it's required by law. You should contact a central notification center at least 48 hours before digging. You simply describe the work site and the type of work you plan to do. Within a day or two, a representative will come to mark the yard to indicate all buried utilities according to a color-coded system. You simply avoid digging in the marked areas.

Call your local utilities provider and have buried gas, water, electric, and sewer lines marked and flagged by a technician before you do any digging.

Planning

Just like projects within the house, one of the chief elements of any outdoor project is its location. The criteria, however, are somewhat different. These criteria include orientation, the presence or absence of sun and shade, and the terrain, as well as setback restrictions and building codes.

Spend some time considering the project itself—what it requires and how it will be maintained. Move on to thinking about (maybe even mapping) the ways you currently use the yard and the space required for those activities.

- A water feature, such as a fountain or water garden, requires access to water. Place it within easy reach of an existing hose bib mounted on your house or plan to run underground water supply lines to it. You can run a garden hose across the yard to fill these features when necessary, but then you have to get one out and put it away each time you need to add water. Adding a dedicated supply line is easier than you may think and is very convenient (see page 219).

- Many outdoor accessories, such as pumps and lighting, require electrical power. Place these amenities within reach of existing receptacles or hire a licensed electrician to hardwire them or run a GFCI-protected, outdoor receptacle to the area. Many such features can be run off heavy-duty extension cords, but doing so requires caution. A cord running across the grass is an open invitation to accidents. Instead, dig a shallow trench for the cord or put it under a thick layer of mulch or gravel. You and your family and guests will be much safer. For an extra layer of protection, lay scrap 1 × 4 or 2 × 4 lumber over the cords in the trench before you bury it.

- Orientation, the direction the feature faces, can be critical to its success. For example, a trellis or arbor on the north side of the house is likely to be shaded most of the day. Not many creeping or trailing vines that are typically grown on these structures thrive in shady conditions, so your choices will be quite limited. On the other hand, placing a feature like this in a sunny spot gives you many, many planting options. It's important to consider orientation when planning water features, too. Sunshine encourages the growth of algae, which increases the maintenance demands of a water garden or other water feature.

- The surrounding terrain has a significant impact on your projects. For example, you wouldn't want to put an artificial turf putting green at a low spot in the yard where water would pool on its surface. Instead, pick a high, level area far enough from trees that the roots won't disturb it and tree debris won't fall on it.

- Be considerate of your neighbors. Don't place a feature that produces noise (a fountain or an activity center like a basketball court) or produces smoke or smells (an outdoor fireplace or kitchen) next to their windows, especially bedroom windows.

Major water features require a dedicated (preferably automatic) water source, but many smaller features can simply be filled on an as-needed basis. The nearer you locate the feature to a spigot, the less work and fuss filling it will entail.

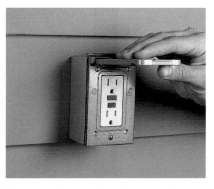

There are several options to choose from to bring power to a remote outdoor location, including extension cords and running a new power line. Whichever you choose, make sure it conforms to local wiring codes.

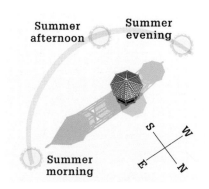

Take note of the way light changes in your yard and anticipate which times of day you're most likely to use a feature as part of the siting process.

If you are planning a feature that is likely to generate noise and activity, be considerate of your neighbors' needs and where their yard features are located.

Establish design breaks within your yard much as you do inside your house. Use fences, hedges, and trellises as walls; use patios, decks, and planting beds as floors. Designate space for dining and entertainment, quiet retreats, and athletic activities.

In your backyard, fences, hedges, and garden walls function like partition walls do inside your house, breaking up larger spaces into more intimate, activity-specific spaces.

Maintenance

One of the most important things you can do to maintain any water feature is to prevent algae and white scale. Research the water treatment options appropriate to your particular feature and the plant and aquatic life in it.

Algae is a living organism that can be prevented by limiting the water's exposure to sunlight and by adding an appropriate water treatment. White scale, which is composed of minerals, is harmful to fish and can be difficult to remove. Many treatments are available to prevent its buildup.

The water levels have to be maintained in any water feature that includes a pump. If the water level falls below the intake valve on the pump, the motor may overheat and burn out. It's best to buy a pump with an override switch to shut off the pump in situations like this, but the problem can also be avoided by simply keeping the water at the recommended level at all times. Water evaporates surprisingly quickly in warm climates, so check the water level at least twice a week. Periodically unplug the pump, remove its cover, and clean the entire unit. Remove debris from the water at the same time.

Occasionally ponds and fountains need to be completely drained and thoroughly cleaned. Silt, debris, and decayed matter build up around the pond, liner, and pump, so all must be disassembled and cleaned.

Drain fountains and replace their water about once a month. At the end of the season, drain the fountain and clean the entire surface, using a household bleach solution.

For putting greens, sweep the surface with a stiff-bristled broom once a week or so. After big storms, remove any twigs or debris that may have blown onto the surface. Once a month or so, hose down the putting green with a garden hose or power washer on a gentle setting.

Installing a Garden Spigot ▸

Extending a water line to a water feature is a very achievable project. Simply run a branch line off your home's water supply system through the foundation or exterior wall and along an underground trench to a hose spigot anchored to a post.

We used copper pipe for the above-ground parts of the run and PE pipe for the buried sections, but local building codes may have different requirements in your area. Be sure to check those codes before beginning this project.

If you live in a severe climate, turn off the water supply and drain the pipes before winter.

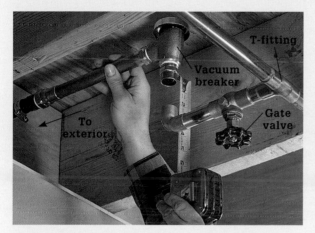

Turn off the water at the main supply valve. Near an exterior wall, cut into a cold water supply pipe and install a T-fitting. Install a straight length of copper, then a gate valve with a bleed fitting. Drill a 1" hole through an exterior wall. Use straight pipe and elbows to extend the branch line through the hole. Install a vacuum breaker at some point along the way.

Dig a trench 8 to 10" wide and 10" deep between the hole where the branch line exits the house and the spigot location. (Slope the trench toward the house at a rate of ⅛" per foot.) Directly below the exit hole, dig a hole for a valve box. Measure, cut, and attach copper pipe and elbows to extend the branch line to the bottom of the trench and out 12". Install a valve box.

At the spigot location, dig a hole big enough for a valve box and a 5-gallon bucket. Create an L-shaped spigot assembly using a 3-ft. copper pipe, a copper elbow, a 2-ft. copper pipe, and a hose spigot. Solder the pieces together. Cut a 1" hole in the side of the bucket and insert the pipe assembly through it. Position the bucket and valve box in the ground. Put a 4 × 4 post into the bucket and use pipe straps to attach the copper assembly to it. Mix quick-drying cement and fill the bucket. Make sure the post is plumb.

Run ¾" PE pipe from the valve box at the house to the valve box at the spigot location. At each valve box, install a T-fitting with a threaded outlet, facing down, onto the PE pipe inside the valve box. Cap the outlet with a plug. At the spigot box, use threaded adapters to join the copper pipe to the PE pipe. Restore the water and test the line for leaks. Fill the trench and replace the sod.

Installing a Backyard Putting Green

Serious golfers often say they "drive for show and putt for dough," and most of them practice putting at every opportunity. For these folks, a backyard putting green is the very definition of luxury.

Natural grass putting greens offer the ultimate in luxurious golf environments at home, but they require special breeds of grass and very specialized maintenance that very few people have the time or equipment to provide. But if you are willing to forego the smell of the fresh-cut Bermuda grass and the feel of a well-tended green underfoot, you'll find that there are a number of artificial putting green options that offer a chance to hone your putting stroke.

The panels and turf we used for this project are available from backyard-putting-greens.com (See Resources page 236). The system is easy to install and produces a good practice surface—a fine combination when it comes to putting greens.

Tools & Materials ▸

Line trimmer	Utility knife	Artificial turf	Spray paint
Heavy scissors	Hammer	Turf spikes	Sand
Screwdriver	Graph paper	Turf tape	Landscape fabric
Jigsaw	Putting green panels	Garden hose or rope	Staples
Spade			

Backyard putting greens give golfers a whole new way to have fun and perfect their game. Special kits, including panels and artificial turf, make building one an easy weekend project.

Designing a Backyard Putting Green

Choose an above-ground green for seasonal use or even to use indoors. They lack a bit of authenticity, but they are very convenient.

Kit accessories, such as pins and edge liners, give a backyard putting green a more genuine flavor. A chipping mat can be positioned around the green to let you work on your close-in short game without destroying your yard. See Resources, page 236.

Artificial turf comes in an array of styles and lengths. Lower nap products, like the two samples to the left, are best for putting greens.

How to Install a Backyard Putting Green

1

2

Diagram your putting green on graph paper, including cup locations. If you are ordering your kit from an Internet seller, they probably have a mapping and planning program on their site. Order panels and turf as necessary to create your putting green.

As soon as it arrives, unroll the turf and spray it with water to saturate. Set the turf aside and let it dry for at least 24 hours. This process preshrinks the turf.

3

4

Measure the installation area and mark the perimeter of the putting green, using a garden hose or rope. Lift the hose or rope and spray-paint the green's outline onto the grass. Some putting green kits are precut to create specific shapes and sizes, while others offer a bit more design flexibility.

Inside the outlined area, use a line trimmer to scalp the grass down to the dirt. Rake up and remove any debris.

Add sand or remove dirt as necessary to create contours in the putting green. Kit manufacturers suggest that you create the contours that replicate the breaks you most want to practice. For example, if you have trouble hitting uphill and to the right, create a hill and place the cup at the top and to the right.

Cover the scalped and contoured installation area with landscape fabric, overlapping seams by at least 2". Trim the fabric to fit inside the outline and secure it to the ground with landscape fabric staples.

Starting in the center of the installation area, push two panels together and hold them tightly in place as you insert the fasteners. Use a screwdriver to tighten the fasteners. Install the panels in locations indicated on your diagram.

Continue to fill in panels, according to your plan. Take special notice of putting cup locations. In many kits, these require special panels with cups preinstalled. Locate them accurately.

(continued)

Where panels go beyond the outline, use a light-colored crayon or chalk to mark a cutting line. Avoid cutting extremely close to panel edges.

One panel at a time, cut panels to shape, using a jigsaw with a blade that's slightly longer than the panel thickness. Use panel scraps to fill in open areas in the layout wherever you can, and then mark and cut the scraps to fit.

Dig a 4"-wide by 4"-deep trench around the perimeter of the green shape, directly next to the edges of the panels.

Unroll the artificial turf on top of the panels. Pay attention to the nap of the turf to make sure it all runs in the same direction. Use a utility knife to cut it to size, 4" larger than the panel assembly.

Install the cups into the panels containing the cup bodies, and then cut holes in the turf with a utility knife.

Fold back the edges of the turf. Apply double-sided carpet tape to the perimeter of the panel assembly. Peel off the tape's protective cover, then press the turf down onto the tape. Fold the excess turf over the edge of the panel assembly and down into the trench. If the turf bulges around a tight radius, make 3½" slashes in the edge of the turf and ease it around the curve.

Drive carpet spikes or fabric spikes (provided by the kit manufacturer) through the edges of the turf and into the trench to secure the turf.

Backfill the trench with the soil you removed earlier. Add landscaping around the edges of the green, if desired. Sweep and hose down the green periodically and as needed.

Installing a Garden Pond & Fountain

A small pond and fountain add more than the illusion of luxury to landscapes; they also add the sound and sparkle of moving water and invite birds to join the party. Installing a pond and fountain can be heavy work, but it's not at all complicated. If you can use a shovel and read a level, you can install a beautiful fountain like the classic Roman fountain shown here.

Most freestanding fountains are designed to be set into an independently installed water feature. The fountains typically are preplumbed with an integral pump, but larger ones may have an external pumping apparatus. The kind of kit you'll find at your local building or garden center normally comes in at least two parts: the pedestal and the vessel.

The project shown here falls into the luxury-you-can-afford category and is fully achievable for a DIYer. If the project you have in mind is of massive scale (with a pond larger than around 8 × 10 ft.) you'll likely need to work with a pondscaping professional to acquire and install the materials needed for such an endeavor.

You can install a fountain in an existing water feature, or you can build a new one with a hard liner, as shown here, or with a soft liner (see pages 232 to 235). Have your utility providers mark the locations of all utility lines before beginning this or any project that involves digging (see page 216).

Tools & Materials ▸

Level	Interlocking
Shovel or spade	paving stones
Hand tamp	Rubber floor mat
Rope	Freestanding fountain
Preformed	Fountain pedestal
pond liner	Tarp
Sand	River stones
Compactable gravel	

The work necessary to install a garden pond and fountain will pay dividends for many years to come. The process is not complicated, but does involve some fairly heavy labor, such as digging and hauling stones.

Installing Ponds & Fountains

Tip ▸

Most municipalities require that permanent water features be surrounded by a structure, fence, or wall on all sides to keep small children from wandering in. Good designers view this as a creative challenge, rather than an impediment.

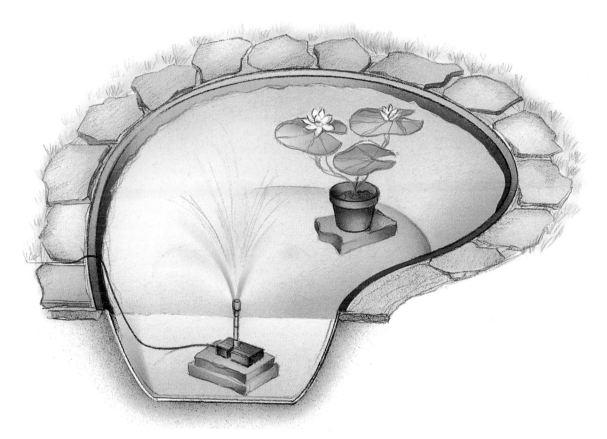

A hard shell-type liner combines well with a fountain because its flat, hard bottom makes a stable surface for resting the fountain base. You may need to prop up the fountain to get it to the optimal level.

If you plan to stock your pond with plant life or livestock, it's important to keep a healthy balance. For stocking with fish, the pond must be at least 24" deep, and you should have at least one submerged water plant to create oxygen.

How to Install a Pond & Fountain

Choose a flat area of your yard. Set the hard-shell pond liner right-side up in the installation area and adjust it until you are pleased with the location (it should be well away from buried utility lines). Hold a level against the edge of the top of the liner and use it as a guide to transfer the liner shape onto the ground below with a rope.

Cut away the sod within the outline. Measure the liner at the center and excavate the base area to this depth. Dig the hole 2 to 3" deeper than the liner, and dig past the outline a couple of inches all the way around. If the sides of your liner are sloped, slope the edges of the hole to match.

Remove any rocks or debris on the bottom of the hole, and add sand to cover the bottom of the hole about 2" deep. Test fit the liner and adjust the sand until the underside of the liner rim is slightly above ground and the liner is level from side to side.

Cut away the sod beyond the liner excavation area and dig out an area wide enough to accommodate your paving stones (called coping stones), about 1" deeper than the average stone thickness. Flagstone is the most common natural stone choice for coping because it is flat; concrete pavers also may be used easily. Make sure the surface of the excavation is as level as possible.

Fill the liner with 4 to 6" of water. Fill the space between the liner and the sides of the hole with damp sand, using a 2 × 4 to tamp it down as you go. Add more water and then more sand; continue until the pond and the gap are filled.

Bail about half of the water out of the pond. Place an exterior rated rubber floor mat (or mats) at least ½" thick on the liner in the spot where you'd like the fountain to rest.

Feed the fountain's power cord up through the access holes in the pedestal. Set the fountain in place on top of the pedestal and run the cord to the edge.

Check to make sure the pedestal is level. If necessary, shim the pedestal with small flat stones to make the fountain level.

(continued)

Cover the pond and pedestal with a clean tarp, and add an inch of compactable gravel to the excavated area for the paving stones. Tamp down the gravel and check the area with a level. Cut a small channel for the power cord and route it beyond the excavated area toward a power source.

Set interlocking pavers in place around lip of liner. Adjust compactable gravel as necessary to make the pavers level.

Ponds look more natural if you line the bottoms with rock. Small-diameter (2 to 3") river rock is a good choice. Before putting it into the pond, rinse the rock well. One trick is to put the nozzle of a hose in the bottom of a clean 5-gallon bucket and then fill the bucket with dirty rock. Turn on the hose and let the water run for 15 minutes or so. This will cause impurities to float up and out of the bucket.

Remove the tarp from the pond and cover the bottom of the liner with washed river rock. Place the fountain onto the pedestal and submerge the cord, running it out of the pond in an inconspicuous spot, such as between two pavers.

Fill both the pond and the fountain's base with water. If you will not be stocking the pond with fish or plants, add two ounces of chlorine bleach for every 10 gallons of water.

Allow the water to settle for 30 minutes or so, and then turn on the fountain pump and test. Let the pump run for an hour or so, and then turn it off and remove the fountain head. Use a hose and spray nozzle to clear out any blockages. Perform this maintenance regularly and whenever you notice that the spray from the fountain seems to be restricted.

Power Cord Management ▶

There are many ways to provide electrical power to operate the fountain pump. The best way is to add a new outdoor circuit, but this requires an electrician if you are not experienced with home wiring. The easier route is to feed your fountain pump with an exterior-rated extension cord that's plugged into an existing outdoor receptacle. Because having an extension cord laying in your lawn is both a

tripping hazard and an electrical hazard (lawn mowers and wiring do not get along), you can bury the cord in a shallow trench. To protect it from digging instruments, either backfill with rocks so you know the exact location of the cord, or bury it encased in heavy conduit.

Avoid using this tactic if the pond is located more than 50 feet from the power source.

Dig a trench about 6" deep and 6" wide from the pond to your outdoor power source.

Feed the cord through conduit and lay the conduit in the trench all the way from the pond to the power source. Backfill the trench with dirt.

Creating a Free-form Meditation Pond

If your idea of a water garden is more elaborate than most or the shape you have in mind isn't standard round or kidney, a free-form water garden with a soft, pliable pond liner may be the answer for you.

Building a water garden with a soft liner is not difficult or time consuming, but the finished garden will require ongoing maintenance and care. Think carefully about your willingness and ability to provide this care before committing yourself to the project. It's also a good idea to look into local building codes—many municipalities require building permits for ponds over 18 inches deep.

Before selecting a flexible liner, compare and contrast the available types. PVC (polyvinyl chloride) liners are made from a type of synthetic vinyl that's flexible and stable as long as it does not get direct sunlight exposure. If you choose one, make sure it is not manufactured for swimming pools or roofing.

EPDM (ethylene propylene diene monomer) liners are made from a synthetic rubber that is highly flexible, extremely durable, and fish-friendly. EPDM liners remain flexible at temperatures ranging from -40°F to 175°F. They are much easier to find, inexpensive, and overall an excellent choice for DIYers. Look for a liner that's at least 45 mil thick. At larger home and garden centers, you can now buy pond liner by the lineal foot.

Tools & Materials ▸

Level	Pond underlayment
Shovel or spade	Flexible pond liner
Hand tamp	Sand
Tape measure	Compactable gravel
Garden hose or rope	Flagstone pavers
Spray paint	

Free-form ponds blend into the landscape, especially with the addition of coping stones set into the edges. Building one involves heavy labor, but no special skills.

How to Create a Free-form Meditation Pond

Flexible liners adapt to nearly any shape or size pond you want. They can fit a typical kidney-shaped excavation with planting shelves, like the one shown here, or a very unique shape of your own design. EPDM rubber liner material is sold in precut sizes at your local home and garden center.

Select a location well away from buried utility lines. Use a garden hose or a rope to outline the pond. Avoid very sharp turns, and try for a natural looking configuration. When you're satisfied with the pond's shape, lift the hose or rope and use spray paint to mark the perimeter.

Find the lowest point on the perimeter and flag it for reference as the elevation benchmark. This represents the top of the pond's water-holding capacity, so all depth measurements should be taken from this point. Start digging at the deepest point (usually the middle of the pond) and work out toward the edges. For border plantings, establish one 6- to 8"-wide ledge about 12" down from the benchmark.

Set a level on the plant shelf to confirm that it is the same elevation throughout. Unless your building site is perfectly level or you have done a lot of earth moving, the edges of the pond are not likely to be at the same elevation, so there may be some pond liner visible between the benchmark and the high point. This can usually be concealed with plants, rocks, or by overhanging your coping more in high areas.

(continued)

Dig a 4"-deep by 12"-wide frame around the top of the hole to make room for the coping stones (adjust the width if you are using larger stones). Remove any rocks, debris, roots, or anything sharp in the hole, and add a 2" layer of sand to cover the bottom.

Cover the bottom and sides of the excavation with pond underlayment. Pond underlayment is a shock-absorbing, woven fabric that you should be able to buy from the same source that provides your liner. If necessary, cut triangles of underlayment and fit them together, overlapping pieces as necessary to cover the contours. This is not a waterproof layer.

Lay out the liner material and let it warm in the sun for an hour or two. Arrange the liner to cover the excavation, folding and overlapping as necessary. Place rocks around the edges to keep it from sliding into the hole.

Begin filling the pond with water. Watch the liner as the water level gets higher, and adjust and tuck it to minimize sharp folds and empty pockets.

Add some larger stones to the pond as the water rises, including a flat stone for your pond pump/filter. If the pump/filter has a fountain feature, locate it near the center. If not, locate it near the edge in an easy-to-reach spot.

Fill the pond all the way to the top until it overflows at the benchmark. Remove the stones holding the liner in place and begin laying flat stones, such as flagstones, around the perimeter of the pond. Cut and trim flagstones as necessary to minimize gaps.

Finish laying the coping stones and fill in gaps with cutoff and shards. If you are in a temperate climate, consider mortaring the coping stones, but be very careful to keep wet mortar out of the water: it kills plants and damages pump/filters. Set flagstone pavers on the ledge at the perimeter of the pond. Add more water and adjust the liner again. Fill the pond to just below the flagstones, and trim the liner.

Consult a garden center, an extension agent from a local university, or the Internet to help you choose plants for your pond. Include a mixture of deep-water plants, marginals, oxygenators, and floating plants. Place the plants in the pond. If necessary to bring them to the right height, set the plants on bricks or flat stones. Spread decorative gravel, sand, or mulch to cover the liner at the perimeter of the pond. Install plants along the pond's margins, if desired.

Resources

Alaco Ladder
888 310 7040
www.alacoladder.com

Armstrong
Flooring and ceiling tiles.
877 276 7876
www.armstrong.com

Apex Wine Cellars & Racking
Manufacturer of wine racks and cooling systems;
     featured on p. 150 to 153.
888 999 9749
www.apexwinecellars.com

Alpine Design Coolers
Available at Sports Authority retail stores

Backyard Golf
Artificial turf putting greens; Muirfield model featured on
     p. 222 to 225.
770 456 5322
www.backyard-golf.com

Bang & Olufsen
Audio, video, and digital media.
866 520 1400
www.bang-olufsen.com

Baums Dancewear
Single and double ballet barres and mounting hardware.
800 832 6246
www.baumsdancewear.com

Behr
Silverscreen paint 770E-2, p.70-71
877 237 6158
www.behr.com

Broan Nutone, LLC
Ventilation, vent/fan/light combinations; featured on
     p. 88 to 91.
262 673 4340
www.broan-nutone.com

Cheap Humidors
888 674 8307
www.cheaphumidors.com

GoFit
Doorway chin-up bars and mounting hardware.
Available at DGS: 800 932 3339
www.gymsupply.com

Hide A Door®
888 771 3667
www.hideadoor.com

Hunter-Douglas
Window fashions.
www.hunterdouglas.com

Jacuzzi Brands
800 288 4002
www.jacuzzi.com

Knape and Vogt
Composite wall mirrors for home gyms.
800 253 1561
www.knapeandvogt.com

Seattle Glass Block, Inc.
485 483 9977
www.seattleglassblock.com

Projector Central
Home theater screens, lamps, ceiling mounts, LCD TVs,
     Plasma TVs, and more.
408 329 4305
www.projectorcentral.com

Projector People
813 261 1512
www.projectorpeople.com

Putnam Rolling Ladder, Co.
212 226 5147
www.putnamrollingladder.com

Putting-Greens.com
978 465 9345
www.putty-greens.com

Rhino Sport, Inc.
Outdoor gym court flooring and artificial turf.
800 585 0922
www.rhinocourts.com

Screen-Tech
Projection screens.
+ 49 4893 373 101
www.screen-tech.de

Therma-Tru
Entry and patio doors.
800 843 7628
www.thermatru.com

Warmrails
Wall-mounted, hard- and soft-wired towel warmers.
877 927 6724 / 714 890 3644
www.warmrails.com

Woodfold Mfg., Inc.
Bookcase door systems; featured on p. 136 to 137.
503 357 7181
www.woodfold.com

Photographers

Linda Oyama Bryan
p. 10 (top & lower left), 21 (lower), 36 (top), 74, 76 (top & lower), 77, 109, 139, 145 (lower) photos © Linda Oyama Bryan for Orren Pickell Designers & Builders; 15 photo © Linda Oyama Bryan for Great Rooms Designers & Builders, Inc.; 140 photo © Linda Oyama for Great Rooms Designers & Builders, Inc.; 173 (lower right) photo © Linda Oyama Bryan for Orren Pickell Designers and Builders

Eric Roth
p. 6 (top right), 8 (lower right), 10 (lower right), 12, 40, 69 (lower), 102, 104 (top & lower), 108, 141 (lower), 144, 173 (lower right), 174 (top right)

Scot Zimmerman
p. 34, 37, 39 (top), 142 (lower right)

Brian Vanden Brink
p. 6 (top left & lower), 11 (top left & right), 14 (lower), 17 (top), 107 (top)

Jackson Hill
p. 46

Through the Lens Management
p. 38 (top) © Thomas McConnell, 105 © Wesley Rose

iStockphoto
www.istockphoto.com
p. 7 (top), © M. Eric Honeycutt; 7 (lower) © Ugur Evirgen; 16 © Eliza Snow, 18 © Michelle Malven; 20 © Sandra O'Claire; 212 (top) © Bruce Shippee, 216 (top) © Karen Locke; 212 (lower) © Franc Podgoreck; 213 (top left) © Alexandra Kostenyuk; 213 (lower) © Kathleen & Scott; 213 (top right) © Elena Elisseeva; 107 (lower) © Urga Rubinovaite; 121 (top) © Fabricio Hernandez; 121 (lower) © Christian Riedel; 120 © Polina Yun; 79 (lower) © Karen Phillips; 17 (lower), © Bojan Tezak; 46 (lower), 106 (top) © Rebecca Ellis; 46 (top) © Alex Slobodkin; 232 © Dan Brandenburg; also p.44, 46, (lower), 147, 210, 215, 221 (top), 232

Apex Wine Cellars & Racking
p. 141 (top), 142 (top), 143

Armstrong
p. 60, 83

Bizo
p. 173 (lower left), 184, 195

Bose
p. 43 (top)

Broan Nutone
p. 79 (top), 91 (top), 147 (top)

Ceramic Tiles of Italy
p. 8 (top), 142 (lower left)

CheapHumidors.com
p. 85 (all)

Finnleo
p. 170, 204

Gaggenau
p. 148, 149

Woodfold Mfg., Inc.
p. 136, 137

Hunter Douglas
p. 43 (lower), 78 (top & lower), 106 (lower) courtesy of Hunter-Douglas window fashions: Heritance® hardwood shutters, Palm Beach™ polysatin shutters, NewStyle® hybrid shutters.

IBS Fireplaces
p. 36 (lower)

Infinity Systems
p. 48

Innovative Theaters
p. 45

Jacuzzi
p. 4, 9, 174 (lower)

Kohler
p. 172 (top left & right), 173 (top), 176

MTI Whirlpools
p. 8 (lower left), 174 (top left), 175 (top & lower)

Nautilus
www.nautilus.com
p. 22, 23

Panasonic
p. 39 (lower) 69 (lower right)

ProSport
p. 220, 214 (top)

Rotel
p. 49

Seattle Glass Blocks
p. 11 (lower), 179 (lower)

Screentech
p. 38 (lower)

SIM2
p. 47

Velux
p. 14 (top), 17 (top), 19 (lower), 21 (lower)

Metric Conversion Charts

Converting Measurements

To Convert:	To:	Multiply by:
Inches	Millimeters	25.4
Inches	Centimeters	2.54
Feet	Meters	0.305
Yards	Meters	0.914
Square inches	Square centimeters	6.45
Square feet	Square meters	0.093
Square yards	Square meters	0.836
Cubic inches	Cubic centimeters	16.4
Cubic feet	Cubic meters	0.0283
Cubic yards	Cubic meters	0.765
Pounds	Kilograms	0.454

To Convert:	To:	Multiply by:
Millimeters	Inches	0.039
Centimeters	Inches	0.394
Meters	Feet	3.28
Meters	Yards	1.09
Square centimeters	Square inches	0.155
Square meters	Square feet	10.8
Square meters	Square yards	1.2
Cubic centimeters	Cubic inches	0.061
Cubic meters	Cubic feet	35.3
Cubic meters	Cubic yards	1.31
Kilograms	Pounds	2.2

Lumber Dimensions

Nominal - U.S.	Actual - U.S. (in inches)	Metric
1 × 2	¾ × 1½	19 × 38 mm
1 × 3	¾ × 2½	19 × 64 mm
1 × 4	¾ × 3½	19 × 89 mm
1 × 5	¾ × 4½	19 × 114 mm
1 × 6	¾ × 5½	19 × 140 mm
1 × 7	¾ × 6¼	19 × 159 mm
1 × 8	¾ × 7¼	19 × 184 mm
1 × 10	¾ × 9¼	19 × 235 mm
1 × 12	¾ × 11¼	19 × 286 mm
2 × 2	1½ × 1½	38 × 38 mm

Nominal - U.S.	Actual - U.S. (in inches)	Metric
2 × 3	1½ × 2½	38 × 64 mm
2 × 4	1½ × 3½	38 × 89 mm
2 × 6	1½ × 5½	38 × 140 mm
2 × 8	1½ × 7¼	38 × 184 mm
2 × 10	1½ × 9¼	38 × 235 mm
2 × 12	1½ × 11¼	38 × 286 mm
4 × 4	3½ × 3½	89 × 89 mm
4 × 6	3½ × 5½	89 × 140 mm
6 × 6	5½ × 5½	140 × 140 mm
8 × 8	7¼ × 7¼	184 × 184 mm

Metric Plywood

Standard Sheathing Grade	Sanded Grade
7.5 mm (⁵/₁₆")	6 mm (⁴/₁₇")
9.5 mm (³/₈")	8 mm (⁵/₁₆")
12.5 mm (½")	11 mm (⁷/₁₆")
15.5 mm (⁵/₈")	14 mm (⁹/₁₆")
18.5 mm (¾")	17 mm (²/₃")
20.5 mm (¹³/₁₆")	19 mm (¾")
22.5 mm (⁷/₈")	21 mm (¹³/₁₆")
25.5 mm (1")	24 mm (¹⁵/₁₆")

Counterbore, Shank & Pilot Hole Diameters

Screw Size	Counterbore Diameter for Screw Head	Clearance Hole for Screw Shank	Pilot Hole Diameter	
			Hard Wood	Soft Wood
#1	.146 (⁹/₆₄)	⁵/₆₄	³/₆₄	¹/₃₂
#2	¼	³/₃₂	³/₆₄	¹/₃₂
#3	¼	⁷/₆₄	¹/₁₆	³/₆₄
#4	¼	⅛	¹/₁₆	³/₆₄
#5	¼	⅛	⁵/₆₄	¹/₁₆
#6	⁵/₁₆	⁹/₆₄	³/₃₂	⁵/₆₄
#7	⁵/₁₆	⁵/₃₂	³/₃₂	⁵/₆₄
#8	³/₈	¹¹/₆₄	⅛	³/₃₂
#9	³/₈	¹¹/₆₄	⅛	³/₃₂
#10	³/₈	³/₁₆	⅛	⁷/₆₄
#11	½	³/₁₆	⁵/₃₂	⁹/₆₄
#12	½	⁷/₃₂	⁹/₆₄	⅛

Index